GRAHAM CHAPMAN   PAUL BUTTERFIELD

HRAN   NAT KING COLE   CLEME

DARIN   JAMES DEAN   JOHN COLTRANE

LLIS   BRIAN EPSTEIN   DIVINE   DOMINIQ

LD   JUDY GARLAND   RAINER WERNER FAS

N   BILLIE HOLIDAY   LOU GEHRIG   LOW

DY   JACK KEROUAC   BUDDY HOLLY   BR

CE LEE   JOHN LENNON   MARTIN LUTHER

ORPE   BOB MARLEY   CAROLE LOMBARD

MARILYN MONROE   CHRISTA MCAULIF

MUNSON   RICK NELSON   KEITH MOON

PARKER   SYLVIA PLATH   PHIL OCHS

ONER   OTIS REDDING   ELVIS PRESLEY

TEVIE RAY VAUGHAN   JESSICA SAVITCH

ILSON   NATALIE WOOD   FATS WALLER

TOO YOUNG TO DIE

PUBLICATIONS INTERNATIONAL, LTD.

Louis Weber, C.E.O.
Publications International, Ltd.
7373 North Cicero Avenue
Lincolnwood, Illinois 60646

ISBN 88176-932-0

Library of Congress Card Catalog Number 91-65675

Contributing Writers:

Dan Kening, a regular contributor to the *Chicago Tribune,* is a pop music writer for *Chicago Magazine* and has written for many other entertainment publications.

David O'Shea is a free-lance writer whose work appears regularly in *American Film Magazine, US,* and *TV Guide.*

Jay Paris, a former editor of *Ohio Magazine,* is a free-lance writer whose work appears frequently in *Reader's Digest, Yankee Magazine,* and the *Boston Globe.*

Photo Credits:

Front cover: **Cinema Collectors:** (left center & center); **Retna:** (right center).

AP/Wide World: 6, 13 (center), 32, 33, 51 (center), 57, 67, 82, 83, 103, 105, 124 (top), 127, 128, 154, 177, 180, 181, 189 (center), 190, 191; **BMI/Michael Ochs Archives:** 26; **Cinema Collectors:** 120 (center), 135, 136, 138, 139, 156, 157, 158, 159, 160 (top); **Culver Pictures:** 56, 58, 155; **Gamma-Liaison:** 185 (center); **Globe Photos:** 9, 10, 13 (top), 24 (center), 29, 43, 50, 51 (top), 52, 53, 54, 64, 69, 80, 87, 91 (center), 94, 95, 96 (center), 97, 98 (center), 99, 100, 102 (top), 104 (top), 106, 107, 113 (top), 116, 143 (center), 150 (center), 163, 166 (top), 171, 183, 184, 185 (top), 192; Jim Anderson: 145 (center); Brian Aris: 140 (center); Brvder Basch: 94; Frank Bez: 143 (top); A. Boot: 125, 126; Toby Byron: 153 (center); John Cameola: 148; Herman Ceonary: 31 (center); Ian Cook: 76, 77; Nicholas DeSciose: 65; Curt Gunther: 22; Y. Kahana: 16; Bob Martin: 93; Lynn McAfee: 18, 147 (center), 174 (top); Bruce V. McBroom: 49; G. Merrin: 17 (center); Russ Meyer: 45 (center); Dick Miller: 28; Bob V. Noble: 186; Don Ornitz: 110 (center); M. J. Pokempner: 14; Richard Robinson: 15; Foto Roinger: 115; Ethan A. Russell: 117; Adam Scull: 75; Marc Sharratt: 79; Paul Slade: 100 (top); Bill Warren 108; G. West: 107 (center); Guy H. White III: 17 (top); **Fred W. McDarrah:** 123, 124 (center), 189 (bottom); **Michael Ochs Archives:** 27, 36, 66 (top), 81 (bottom), 85, 86, 149, 151, 152, 153 (top), 167, 168, 176, 178, 179, 182; **Personality Photos, Inc./Howard Frank Archive:** 44 (top); **Photofest:** 5, 7, 11 (top), 12, 19, 20, 25, 30, 31 (top), 34, 35, 37, 38, 39, 40, 41, 45 (top), 46 (bottom), 47, 48, 55, 59, 60 (center), 61, 63, 66, (center), 70, 71, 73, 78, 84, 88, 89, 90, 91 (bottom), 92, 96 (bottom), 98 (top), 101, 102 (center), 109, 110 (top), 111, 112, 113 (bottom), 114, 118, 119, 120 (top), 121, 122, 129, 130, 133 (top), 140 (bottom), 142, 144, 145 (top), 146, 147 (top), 162, 165, 166 (center), 169, 172, 173, 175, 187, 188; Cranston & Elkins: 24 (top); Eileen Darby: 81 (top); Richard Lewis: 23; **Rex Features/Donald Cooper:** 115 (bottom); **Springer/Bettmann Film Archive:** 131, 132; **T.V. Sports Mailbag:** 68; **Universal City Studios:** 11 (bottom), 21; **Warner Bros.:** 42, 72, 74, 133 (bottom), 134, 160 (bottom), 164.

■ CONTENTS ■

During a bleak November weekend, a stunned nation united in front of millions of television screens to mourn John Kennedy, the dashing young president cruelly struck down by an assassin's bullets. On a cold winter afternoon in Central Park's Sheep Meadow, thousands of men and women gathered silently to remember John Lennon in a place that had often pulsed with the super-amplified sounds of be-ins and rock concerts. For many years her doting ex-husband kept fresh red roses in a vase on Marilyn Monroe's crypt, expressing an undying love that is shared by millions of people who knew her only through movies and photographs. Most of us never shook hands with Jack, John, or Marilyn, but when they died young, we mourned them as if they were family and we go on missing their presence in our lives as though they had been dear friends.

The death of any young person is especially poignant, but when a famous person dies young, we feel the loss keenly. A career pointing toward greatness will never come to fruition. The unfulfilled potential of Janis Joplin, Thurmon Munson, Jim Henson, or Martin Luther King Jr. leaves us with wistful thoughts of what might have been.

We will always remember what we were doing when we heard that Elvis had died or that Bobby Kennedy had been shot. We continue to ask ourselves how could Superman kill himself? Why would anyone want to murder Sal Mineo? Why was Natalie Wood swimming alone? Couldn't James Dean simply slow down? Why didn't Jim Henson go to the hospital sooner?

We can guess at the answers. We can speculate about what might have happened if Malcolm X had become a national leader or if Gilda Radner had recovered from cancer. We also can honor the accomplishments of these young people. Putting aside wistful musings about what might have been, this book celebrates the successes of short lives lived to the fullest. The accomplishments of these 74 men and women in sports, civil rights, movies, country, jazz, blues, soul, and rock music, art and literature, television, and politics speak for themselves.

They may have died young, but they are remembered for their courage and their commitment to the vigorous pursuit of life.

On Christmas morning in 1960, 14-year-old Howard Duane Allman was given his first motorcycle. His little brother, Gregg, got a guitar. Gregg soon learned to make music; Duane wrecked his cycle, but he salvaged parts from the broken bike and traded them for a guitar of his own. Within a year the Allman brothers were playing at sock hops in Daytona Beach, Florida, and calling themselves the Kings. They played with other local bands until 1965, when they formed the Allman Joys. The group toured the South, cut a single, but failed to impress anyone.

Duane drifted out to Los Angeles with a new band called Hour Glass. After recording two albums for Liberty Records, Duane returned to Florida. He started playing with the Second Coming in Jacksonville but also traveled frequently to Muscle Shoals, Alabama, home of Rick Hall's Fame Studios. Backing up such greats as Aretha Franklin, King Curtis, and Percy Sledge, Duane made a name for himself as an extraordinary session guitarist. At Duane's suggestion Wilson Pickett recorded Lennon and McCartney's "Hey Jude," with Allman's guitar giving credence to the performance.

In 1969 Duane got the break he had been hoping for. Jerry Wexler, vice-president of Atlantic Records, offered him a solo contract. Allman pulled together a new band with drummers Jai Johanny Johanson and Butch Trucks, guitarist Dickey Betts, bassist Berry Oakley, and brother Gregg on keyboards. Once assembled, the Allman Brothers Band settled in Macon, Georgia, where Phil Walden was setting up Capricorn Records.

The band's first album blends strains of blues, soul, rock, and country into the electrifying sound that launched Southern rock music. As their second album, *Idlewild South*, climbed the charts, the Allman Brothers were tapped to play at New York's Fillmore East, the rock mecca of moment. During their concert there in March 1971, the band recorded a double album. It was released in July and eventually reached the top ten, but Duane did not live long enough to see his band regularly called America's best rock 'n' roll group.

On October 29, 1971, Duane Allman was riding his motorcycle down Macon Street when a tractor trailer pulled in front of him. He lost control of the bike, trying to avoid a collision. The band played at Duane's funeral. Only a year later, they gathered somberly again to bury Berry Oakley, who had been killed in a motorcycle crash just three blocks from the site of Duane's fatal accident.

1946-1971

Duane Allman shaped the engaging new sound of the early Allman Brothers Band with his masterful slide work, which interacted powerfully with Dickey Betts' forceful technique.

1951-1991

Republican party strategist Lee Atwater played a significant role in shaping the tactics George Bush used during his presidential campaign in 1988.

Not long after he was appointed chairman of the Republican National Committee, Lee and the president accompanied the band during a blues concert in Washington.

Few men in politics have been equally celebrated and reviled to the same extent as political strategist Lee Atwater. As manager of the Republican presidential campaign, he organized the dirty but successful strategy George Bush used against Michael Dukakis in the 1988 election. Bush's victory was the crowning achievement of Atwater's career.

Lee was born on February 27, 1951, into a middle-class South Carolina family. He was a poor student in high school but began to flourish intellectually at the state's Newberry College. After his freshman year, his mother got him a job as an intern for Senator Strom Thurmond. Lee traveled throughout South Carolina with Thurmond, learning the basics of Republican politics. After graduating from college, Lee became the executive director of the College Republicans in Washington, D.C. There he first met George Bush, who was then the chairman of the Republican National Committee. Bush won Lee's lifelong friendship when he lent Lee his boat to impress a date, Sally Dunbar, who eventually married Atwater.

In early 1974 Lee returned to South Carolina, where he managed the ill-fated GOP gubernatorial primary campaign of the former Vietnam War commander General William Westmoreland. In 1978 Lee's mentor Strom Thurmond hired him to manage his Senate reelection campaign. Lee's "dirty tricks" tactics against challenger Charles Ravenal earned him national notoriety.

Glib, candid, and colorful, Lee quickly moved up through the political ranks, serving as the Southern coordinator for the 1980 Reagan-Bush campaign. He was the deputy national manager for their equally successful 1984 campaign. His specialty was converting disgruntled Democrats to the GOP by using such issues as crime, school prayer, gay rights, and abortion. In 1988 he managed the Bush-Quayle campaign. His infamous exploitation of the case of Massachusetts murderer-rapist Willie Horton helped defeat Massachusetts governor Dukakis. After the election Bush rewarded Atwater by choosing him to head the Republican National Committee.

In March 1990 Lee was hospitalized following a seizure. He was diagnosed as having brain cancer. After battling his illness for a year, Lee died on March 29, 1991, at a Washington, D.C. hospital. He was 40 years old.

Motown Records achieved phenomenal success during the 1960s, and the label's top group, the Supremes, with Diana Ross, Florence Ballard, and Mary Wilson, were among the era's biggest stars. While Diana went on to succeed as a solo star, Flo's life after she left the Supremes was filled with heartbreak and tragedy.

Flo was born on June 30, 1943. She grew up with Diana and Mary in Detroit's Brewster public housing project. In 1959 the trio began singing together as the Primettes. A few years later, when Motown's president Berry Gordy discovered them, they were already calling themselves the Supremes.

Under Gordy's watchful eye, the girls became stars. After "Where Did Our Love Go" hit the top of the charts in 1964, the Supremes racked up an amazing record of 12 number-one hits. During those heady times, lead singer Diana was the group's focal point, but Flo was the crowd pleaser, who was known for her humorous ad libbing.

By 1967 Diana's ambition could no longer be ignored, and the group was now billed as Diana Ross and the Supremes. Gordy repeatedly called Flo on the carpet for her drinking and her ballooning weight. Late in 1967, he finally fired her from the group. A heartbroken Flo briefly attempted a solo career, but she was barred from billing herself as a former Supreme and got few bookings. Cut off from Diana, Flo occasionally contacted Mary Wilson, who kept the Supremes going after Diana left the group in 1969.

For Flo the beginning of the end was losing her house in Detroit in 1974. She went on welfare and was forced to move with her three daughters back into the Brewster project. Later that year, Mary flew her out to Los Angeles, where she was introduced at a Supremes' concert and received a standing ovation. Shortly after this, $50,000 was mysteriously deposited in her bank account. Some people say Diana was her benefactress. Flo immediately bought a new house and a new Cadillac, and splurged on expensive Christmas presents for her daughters. But her happiness was short lived. She died of cardiac arrest on February 22, 1976, at the age of 32. Her mother, Lurlee, felt that she knew the true cause of Flo's early death: "I think she really died of a broken heart."

1943-1976

During the good times, while the original Supremes were still together, Diana Ross (right) and Mary Wilson (center) always credited Florence Ballard (left) with founding the dynamic trio.

This publicity photograph was taken in 1965 at the height of the Supremes' fame.

1949-1982

In 1978 John Belushi starred in
*National Lampoon's Animal
House,* a tasteless but funny
movie set in a small college
town in the early 1960s.

The comic genius of John Belushi lives on in the samurai butcher from *Saturday Night Live,* the rhythm-and-blues-loving hipster Joliet Jake Blues from *The Blues Brothers,* and the frat boy from Hell, Bluto, in *National Lampoon's Animal House.* A larger-than-life talent with a self-destructive streak to match, John's aggressive "take no prisoners" style has influenced the generation of comedians and actors who grew up watching him on *Saturday Night Live.* John's younger brother, Jim Belushi, carries on the family name, but watching his talent develop and mature, you cannot help wondering what new heights John Belushi might have reached if he had had more time.

The son of an Albanian immigrant restaurant owner, Adam Belushi, and his wife, the vivacious Agnes, John was born in Chicago. He grew up in suburban Wheaton, where the family moved when John was six. Perhaps he was overcompensating for his status as the first male Belushi born in America, but John became the perfect all-American boy during his high-school years. The cocaptain of the Wheaton Central High School football team, he was elected his school's homecoming king his senior year. He also developed an interest in acting and appeared in the high school variety show.

Encouraged by his drama coach, John put aside his plans to become a football coach and decided to pursue acting. After graduation in 1967, he joined a summer stock theatre troupe in rural Indiana. That summer John played a variety of roles from Cardinal Wolsey in *Anne of a Thousand Days* to a hipster jazz man in *The Tender Trap.*

In the fall John started his freshman year at the University of Wisconsin at Whitewater. He grew his hair long and started attending more anti-Vietnam War rallies than classes. Dropping out of Wisconsin, John spent the next two years at the College of DuPage, a junior college a few miles from his parents' Wheaton home. His father was pressuring him to become a partner in his restaurant, but John stuck to his guns about acting.

While he was attending DuPage, John helped found the West Compass Players, an improvisational comedy troupe patterned after Chicago's famous Second City ensemble. By 1971 he made the leap to Second City itself, where he joined a cast that included Harold Ramis (*Ghostbusters*), Joe Flaherty (*SCTV*), and Brian Doyle-Murray (*Saturday Night Live*).

In this scene from *Saturday Night Live,* John hides his signature samurai butcher's pigtail with a baseball cap and visits a psychiatrist's office, where he finds no solutions to his emotional problems.

John and Judy Belushi were married in 1977. They had been high-school sweethearts and were still married at the time of John's death, even though Judy was worried and angered by John's constant heavy drug use.

John loved his life at Second City. He performed six nights a week, perfecting the physical "gonzo" style of comedy he made famous on *Saturday Night Live*. Soon, he was ready to move on, and within a year, John and his high-school sweetheart, Judy Jacklin, were living in New York. John had joined the cast of *National Lampoon's Lemmings,* an off-Broadway rock musical revue that was originally booked for a six-week run but played to capacity audiences for 10 months. John's performance was singled out by a reviewer for the *New Yorker,* who labeled him "a real discovery."

In 1973 John was hired as a writer and actor for the syndicated *National Lampoon Radio Hour.* Along with the *National Lampoon Show* staged the following year, the radio show was a prototype for the Not Ready for Prime Time Players on *Saturday Night Live.*

The Lampoon spinoffs brought John many fans, but in 1975 the groundbreaking television series *Saturday Night Live* made him a star. The aggressively physical style of humor he had begun to develop at Second City flowered on SNL, where Belushi portrayed an angry killer bee with the same intensity he brought to his impressions of Marlon Brando or Joe Cocker.

In 1978 John had a small part in the movie *Goin' South,* directed by and starring Jack Nicholson. That part was just a warmup for his classic role as the beer-swilling Bluto in *National Lampoon's Animal House,* the year's top-grossing comedy. John's performance stole the movie, which portrays fraternity house shenanigans at a small college in the early 1960s. Bluto's rallying cry, "Toga, Toga, Toga," became the anthem of John's growing legions of fans. That year, he also had a smaller and more serious role in another movie, *Old Boyfriends.*

In 1979, after four years in the cast, John quit SNL to devote himself to making movies. He and his best friend Dan Aykroyd appeared as pilots in Steven Spielberg's relatively unsuccessful *1941.* Around this time John's drug use escalated. Cocaine, which was ubiquitous in show-business circles in the late 1970s, was John's drug of choice. His recurrent cocaine binges became a source of friction between John and Judy, whom he had married in 1977.

John's love for blues and soul music inspired the Blues Brothers. He and Aykroyd first appeared as Joliet Jake and Elwood Blues, a pair of white soul men dressed in black suits with skinny ties, pork-pie hats, and Rayban sunglasses, in a skit on SNL. Backed by some of the best musicians in the business, their recreations of 1960s soul classics by Sam and Dave, Otis Redding, and James Brown rocketed the first Blues Brothers album, *A Briefcase Full of Blues,* to the top of the record charts in 1980.

Building on the success of the album, John made the movie *The Blues Brothers,* directed by John Landis. Filmed on location in John's home territory, Chicago, the movie gave him a chance to feature some of his musical heroes, including Ray Charles, Aretha Franklin, and James Brown. Belushi also opened a private club, the Blues Bar, for the duration of the shooting. This gave him, Aykroyd, and the rest of the cast a place to blow off steam at the end of a long day of shooting. Landis said of John at the time, "If he doesn't burn himself out, his potential is unlimited."

John's reputation as an off-screen party animal is legendary, but his generous side is less well known. He bought his father a ranch outside San Diego, where the senior Belushi could realize his lifelong dream to be a cowboy. John helped set up some of his Chicago buddies in their own businesses and kept a close eye on brother Jim, who had followed his path through both Second City and *Saturday Night Live.*

John got good reviews in his next two movies, but neither one did great business at the box office. In *Continental Divide* he played a hard-boiled Chicago newspaper columnist who finds romance in Colorado with eagle expert Blair Brown. He and Aykroyd appeared together once again in the 1981 movie *Neighbors,* which gave them a chance to reverse roles: John was the stable family man whose life is turned upside down when wild man Aykroyd moves in next door.

In 1982 John began work on the screenplay for his next movie, *Noble Rot.* In early March he checked into a bungalow at the Chateau Marmont, a popular celebrity hotel in Los Angeles. His steady use of cocaine in recent weeks had alarmed his family and friends, but he continued to promise his wife that he would quit drugs once and for all.

John Belushi was found dead in his room on March 5, 1982. The Los Angeles coroner's office gave the cause of death as a lethal injection of both cocaine and heroin. Several years later, his companion during his last few days, Cathy Smith, was sentenced to three years in prison for injecting him with the drugs. Close friend James Taylor sang "That Lonesome Road" at a service at the Martha's Vineyard cemetery where John is buried. He was 33 years old.

Roaches, land sharks, and other animals found their way into SNL sketches, but the killer bees were a regular feature of the program, with John portraying the angriest bee of them all.

In the 1980 movie *The Blues Brothers*, John as Joliet Jake Blues and Dan Aykroyd as Elwood Blues attempt to raise $5,000 for an orphanage and cause about $50 million in property damage.

Some people feel that Lenny Bruce was a pioneer comedian who lampooned society's problems. Other people feel he was a foul-mouthed exponent of "sick" humor. Either way, the controversial comedian became a legend after his death, inspiring books, plays, and a feature film about his life and times.

Lenny Bruce started life as Leonard Alfred Schneider on October 13, 1925, in Mineola, Long Island. His English-born father, Myron, was a podiatrist. His mother, Sadie, was a dancer who used the stage name Sally Marr. Lenny's parents divorced when he was five. To support herself and her child, Sadie continued her dancing career, sending Lenny to stay with various aunts, uncles, and grandparents. Later, he wrote in his autobiography, *How to Talk Dirty and Influence People:* "My childhood wasn't exactly an Andy Hardy movie."

1925-1966

Lenny Bruce was detained for two hours at the airport when he arrived in London on April 8, 1963, and then sent back to Idlewild Airport in New York.

Although he dropped out of high school, Lenny was an avid reader and largely educated himself. He enlisted in the Navy in 1942, but he won a discharge by convincing a team of Navy psychiatrists that he was a homosexual. With some help from his mother, Lenny began doing impressions, one liners, and movie parodies in nightclubs. In 1948 he was "discovered" on the television show *Arthur Godfrey's Talent Scouts.* In 1951 the budding comedian married Honey Harlowe, a red-haired stripper. The marriage broke up five years later, and after Honey was busted for a narcotics violation, Lenny raised their daughter, Kitty, by himself.

Lenny began to work his way up from seedy strip joints and jazz clubs. In his act he was a dark, slender, and intense figure who prowled the stage like a caged animal and spoke into a hand-held microphone. His monologues were peppered with four-letter words and Yiddish expressions. Lenny lampooned racism by forcing his audiences to examine their own racial prejudices. In one famous routine, he asked, "Are there any niggers here tonight?"

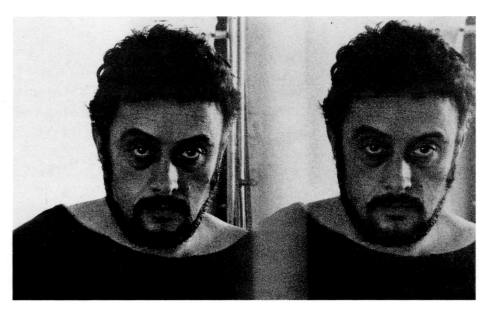

Toward the end of his life, Lenny spent most of his time alone in his apartment writing. This photograph was taken during those bleak days.

Lenny Bruce directed his considerable wit and humor against the hypocrisy of the times in which he lived. Unfortunately, the hypocrisy he hoped to debunk eventually destroyed first his career and then Lenny himself.

and then proceeded to count the number of "kikes, spics, and guineas" in the house. Another of his favorite targets was organized religion. In "Religions, Inc." he acted out a conversation between Oral Roberts and the pope, with both men talking in the vernacular of glib show-business personalities.

Through his nightclub appearances and record albums, Lenny became the hipster saint of the comedy world, crossing the line of propriety where others feared to tread. By the early 1960s, he began to take on the persona of a prophet as much as a standup comedian. "Sometimes I see myself as a profound, incisive wit, concerned with man's inhumanity to man," he once said. "Then I stroll to the next mirror, and I see a pompous, subjective ass."

In 1964 Bruce was arrested on an obscenity charge following a New York club appearance. As he listened to a police inspector read from his notes about his performance, Lenny said, "Listen to him. He loves doing my act." Despite testimony on his behalf by noted writers, critics, educators, and politicians, Lenny was found guilty.

Continually harassed by the police, Lenny became depressed and paranoid. Further prosecutions for obscenity and narcotics charges drove him closer to instability. By 1965 he was broke and $40,000 in debt. He claimed that every time he got a gig the police would threaten to arrest the club owner if he let Lenny go onstage. In February 1966 Lenny played Los Angeles for the first time in several years. Bearded, flabby, and haggard, he performed for a small crowd that included several hecklers and some vice-squad detectives. His performance centered on his current obsessions: his constitutional right of free speech, free assembly, and freedom from unreasonable searches and seizures. When a friend asked him why he had turned his back on comedy, he said, "I'm not a comedian anymore. I'm Lenny Bruce."

On August 3, 1966, Lenny was found lying naked on the bathroom floor of his Hollywood home, with a hypodermic needle stuck in one arm. He was dead from a narcotics overdose at the age of 40.

British authorities felt it was in the public interest to refuse Lenny Bruce permission to enter Great Britain. The comedian's V-sign salute was his ironic response.

1942-1987

Growing up in Chicago, Paul Butterfield learned to play flawless blues harmonica by jamming with some of the all-time great blues men.

Paul Butterfield and Mike Bloomfield, along with other members of Paul's band, backed Bob Dylan at Newport for his controversial first electric performance.

Paul Butterfield was a Chicago blues man whose band renewed interest in the kind of American music known as the blues in the years following the British Invasion of the music scene in the United States. He was born on December 17, 1942, and studied classical flute for 10 years. During high school Paul took up the harmonica, and by the time he was 16, he was playing in some of Chicago's best South Side blues clubs. Such blues legends as Howlin' Wolf and Little Walter let Butterfield jam with them. His fiery solos awed the audience. How could a skinny white kid play the blues with the same fervor as an old-time black blues man from Mississippi?

Paul attended the University of Chicago, where he met Elvin Bishop. Together they formed the six-member Butterfield Blues Band. In the mid 1960s, they were one of the most popular and controversial bands in Chicago. The controversy centered around the belief of blues traditionalists that using amplification and blending folk, jazz, and rock with the blues was heresy. Butterfield's band was not a blues band according to traditionalists, but the kids who flocked to the group's concerts could have cared less.

The record companies also took notice. In 1965 *Butterfield Blues Band* was released on the Elektra label. Guitarist Mike Bloomfield joined the group for the recording sessions. At the Newport Folk Festival in Rhode Island, Butterfield's band blew the house down, stealing the show from Bob Dylan. The band was gaining a good reputation, but they were not yet nationally known stars.

In 1967 the band was transformed by the addition of horns. Charles Dinwiddie on tenor sax, Keith Johnson on trumpet, and David Sanborn on alto sax made up the expanded lineup. This version of the band released two albums. They were critically well received but did not sell especially well. Bishop left the group in 1968, and Butterfield attempted to reorganize his band. By 1971 only Sanborn and Dinwiddie were left. Playing with this band, Butterfield achieved a large cult following.

In 1972 Paul decided to make a serious attempt to appeal to the largest possible audience. The Butterfield Blues Band became Paul Butterfield's

Better Days. From 1972 until 1981, the group recorded for the Bearsville label. The band made several albums but none was very successful, so Paul again changed his lineup.

In 1981 Paul was stricken by an attack of diverticulitis, which caused his intestines to burst. His serious illness kept him away from playing for four long years. When Butterfield tried to return to the studio, he encountered financial problems. Bearsville would not fund his project. Eventually, he found backing from Amherst Records of Buffalo, New York. *Paul Butterfield Rides Again* was released in 1986.

Paul Butterfield was found dead in his North Hollywood apartment on May 4, 1987. His friends felt that he had died because there was just no more fight left in him. "His music was all he ever had," said Bishop. Although Butterfield did not reach the kind of audience he would have liked, he influenced several great blues men, including Robert Cray and Stevie Ray Vaughan. Butterfield may have never sold a million records, but he honed his craft and passed it along to other musicians.

In 1972 Paul moved to Woodstock, New York, where he formed Paul Butterfield's Better Days, shown here at a recording session.

1950-1983

Karen Carpenter's remarkably clear voice blended with her brother's mellow tones to create a unique sound that was well suited to the excellent material the duo recorded.

The song title chosen as the name for the 1971 television variety series Karen Carpenter hosted with her brother expresses the theme of Karen's short career, *Make Your Own Kind of Music*. Bucking current trends to join rock and pop, the Carpenters created a densely layered sound that was entirely their own.

Karen was born in New Haven, Connecticut, on March 2, 1950. In 1963 her family moved to Downey, California. Before the move her brother Richard, who had begun playing piano when he was nine, had been taking lessons at Yale. In California the music in the Carpenter household was dominated by what Karen called "the three Bs": the Beatles, the Beach Boys, and Burt Bacharach. Karen wanted to be a drummer, and the only formal training she ever received was with her high school's marching band.

In 1965 Richard decided to put together an instrumental trio, with Karen on drums and their friend Wes Jacobs on bass and tuba. Karen was only 16 years old when the group competed in a battle of the bands at the Hollywood Bowl. She was really reluctant about playing, but as often happened, Karen's parents and brother urged her to go ahead and perform. The group won first place and a recording contract with RCA.

After cutting two LPs that were never released, the trio broke up. Karen formed a band of her own with four other students from Cal State. The group called itself Spectrum, sang harmony very well, and played several local gigs before disbanding.

Karen and Richard made several demo tapes in a friend's garage. Richard overdubbed the tapes creating a unique sound, which eventually came to the attention of Herb Alpert. He liked what he heard and offered the Carpenters a contract with A&M. Borrowing from their three Bs, the Carpenters' first hit was a reworking of the Beatles' "Ticket to Ride." Then they recorded Bacharach's "Close to You"; it sold a million copies in 1970. Add to an ever-increasing list of hit singles an Academy Award, a world tour, and a television series, and the Carpenters became one of the most successful groups of the early 1970s. For Karen the high point of those heady years was an invitation to the White House. President Nixon asked the Carpenters to perform at a state dinner honoring West German leader Willy Brandt on May 1, 1974. The president told them they were "young America at its very best."

To the president and her other fans, Karen may have looked as though she were on top of the world. But she was suffering from anorexia nervosa, a mental illness characterized by obsessive dieting. In 1975 the Carpenters were forced to cancel a European tour because Karen was too weak to perform. Struggling to take control of her life, at the age of 26 (in 1976), Karen moved out of her parents' home and into a nearby apartment.

In 1980 she married a real estate developer named Thomas J. Burris. The next year she and her brother were back in the recording studio. Their 1981 LP, *Made in America,* had several hit singles, including "Touch Me

Although she had little formal training, Karen became a strong drummer, who seemed at home behind her kit.

Karen was not a natural performer. From her first appearance in competition at the Hollywood Bowl throughout her career, she needed a lot of encouragement from her brother and parents to urge her onto the stage.

When We're Dancing." But Karen was unable to shake her deepening depression. She spent most of 1982 in a New York City hospital undergoing treatment. By then her marriage had fallen apart, and Karen began divorce proceedings.

Karen started 1983 with renewed hope. She had gained weight and was planing to return to the studio. For the first time in several years, she was making public appearances. This was one of the few times since she became a professional recording artist that Karen felt really good about herself.

On February 4, 1983, Karen went over to her parents' house to sort through the wardrobe she kept there. Karen was in a walk-in closet when, without warning, she collapsed from cardiac arrest. Karen Carpenter was pronounced dead later that same day. The doctors said that her long battle with anorexia nervosa had stressed her heart.

1942-1981

A tireless performer, Harry Chapin booked 200 concerts a year, more than half of which were charity gigs that raised millions of dollars for worthy causes.

Unlike many folk-rock stars, Harry Chapin continued to play acoustic guitar throughout the 1970s.

Without the hard work of Harry Chapin, the Presidential Commission on Hunger might never have been created. For several years Chapin lobbied on Capitol Hill and barraged the president with requests that he do something about America's hungry people. Finally, in 1978, Jimmy Carter agreed to establish the commission, but he insisted that Chapin continue to be actively involved. The president also requested that the activist performer report directly to him, which naturally Chapin was only too glad to do.

Harry cared deeply about people. He liked ordinary folks and did not pal around with other stars. He sang about the things he believed and the people he cared about. Most of Chapin's folk ballads recount the stories of regular people, from taxi drivers and factory workers to estranged lovers.

Chapin was born on December 7, 1942. His family was not working class, as you might expect from his music. His dad was the jazz drummer "Big Jim" Chapin, and his grandfather was the noted philosopher and literary critic Kenneth Burke. Chapin's family was close-knit and musical. When he was just a little kid, Harry played trumpet and guitar with his brothers, Steve and Tom, around their Brooklyn Heights neighborhood in New York City. The family act disbanded temporarily when Harry decided to attend the Air Force Academy. When that did not work out, he completed his college education with a semester at Cornell University, where he studied filmmaking.

Music may have been Harry's first love, but he always had many other interests. He flew airplanes, played pool like an expert, and made movies. *Legendary Champions,* a documentary about boxing, earned a 1969 Oscar nomination. That same year, Harry also directed and wrote the score for another documentary, *Blue Water, White Shark.*

While he was making movies, Harry was also playing in Greenwich Village with a band that included his brothers and sporadically his father. For a short time, he also appeared with his brother Tom in a group called Brothers and Sisters, along with Carly and Lucy Simon. His debut album, *Heads and Tales,* was released in 1972. With his album on the charts and his song "Taxi" in the top 40, Harry was nominated for a Grammy for Best New Artist.

Chapin produced 10 albums during the 1970s, but this multitalented performer was never content to repeat past successes. In 1975 he wrote and

Harry and his wife lived happily together on Long Island, where Harry was an active supporter of an arts organization in addition to the many other causes he championed.

starred in a multimedia Broadway show, *The Night That Made America Famous.* That same year, he also wrote a book, *Looking . . . Seeing.* Along with everything else he was doing, for five years Harry also coproduced and coauthored some of the music for his brother Tom's children's television series, *Make a Wish.* Most important to Chapin were his tireless efforts toward helping the world's poor. He served on the boards of directors of many not-for-profit organizations. Harry also gave much of the income from his album sales and his 200 yearly concert appearances to charity.

In 1981 he had released his eleventh album, *Sequel,* and was planning to produce a ballet set to his music. On July 16 Harry was traveling along the Long Island Expressway on his way to a business meeting. An erratic driver, whose license had been suspended several times, slammed into his car. Harry Chapin was killed instantly.

Thirteen members of the House of Representatives eulogized him for his contributions as a humanitarian. Consumer activist Ralph Nader suggested that Chapin allowed his generosity and good will to impede his own career: "People in the music business often condescend to those who sing too much for free." Nader went on to call Harry a modern-day hero. If he were alive today, Harry would have participated in We Are the World and other projects that help hungry people. Without his early efforts, these events, which the music industry now considers fashionable, might never have taken place.

1941-1989

In one of his hilarious roles on the Monty Python television series, Graham Chapman dons a military uniform and proceeds to act nutty.

Even in the company of the five other eccentrics who made up Monty Python, Graham Chapman stood out—all six feet four inches of him. A medical doctor with a degree from Cambridge, he was openly gay long before it was socially acceptable. Graham was always uniquely himself, always his own man. On the Monty Python television series, he often portrayed poker-faced upper-class twits, who were the brunt of the other Pythons' jokes. John Cleese and Eric Idle usually got the funnier parts and most of the glory, but as Cleese said later, Chapman was "probably the most talented actor of us all."

Graham was born in Leicester, England, on January 8, 1941, while a Nazi blitz was in full swing over the town. His father was a police inspector and probably inspired the constables Graham so often portrayed in Python sketches. Graham studied medicine in college and earned an M.D., but he never tried to earn a living as a doctor. At Cambridge he took part in a series of comedy revues, and by the time he graduated, he knew what he wanted to do with his life.

In 1969, along with Cleese, Idle, Michael Palin, Terry Jones, and Terry Gilliam, Graham formed the comedy group Monty Python. Their BBC television series, *Monty Python's Flying Circus,* was an instant hit. Their off-kilter, inherently English style of humor was delightfully original but completely accessible. For Graham and the rest of the Pythons, there were no sacred cows—not politicians, not the royal family, and certainly not Britain's imperial past. Before the show appeared on public television, many people assumed that Americans would find Monty Python much too British to be funny. But PBS had never had a larger audience than when stations began to rerun the old Python shows beginning in the mid 1970s. The classic Python routines have become standard college humor. People know entire sketches, such as the "Pet Shop," "Argument Clinic," or "Crunchy Frog," and almost every student knows a chorus of the lumberjack or Spam songs.

The Pythons' movies, which did very well at the box office when they were first released, are also cult favorites. Graham played the title role in the 1979 movie *The Life of Brian* in which he is delightfully sweet and simple minded. He is also a not-so-masterful King Arthur in the group's earlier movie, *Monty Python and the Holy Grail.*

It may seem ironic that Graham was part of a comedy troupe that often made jokes about "queers" and "pooftahs," but Python's humor was always genuinely funny and not homophobic. Chapman never tried to hide his homosexuality and was open about his long-term relationship with writer David Sherlock. They were together for 24 years, including all the time Chapman was with Monty Python. Graham was a cofounder of Britain's *Gay News.* He also adopted and raised a teenage runaway, John Tomiczek.

By the late 1970s, most of the Pythons were pursuing independent projects. In 1983 Graham wrote and starred in the movie *Yellowbeard,* which received largely negative reviews. In 1988 with his companion, David

In the 1983 movie *Monty Python's the Meaning of Life*, John Cleese is the headmaster, and from left to right, Eric Idle, Michael Palin, Graham Chapman, and Terry Jones are his students.

Sherlock, he cowrote and starred in the short-lived CBS-TV series *Jake's Journey.* In the show he played a wizard who takes a young boy on fantastic adventures in time.

A longtime alcoholic, who suffered liver damage before he stopped drinking in 1977, Graham's health went into decline in 1988. A routine visit to his dentist revealed a tumor on his tonsil. Another tumor on his spine later confined him to a wheelchair. Graham underwent a series of operations as well as radiation therapy. Whenever he was hospitalized, he had to deny rumors that his illness was the result of AIDS.

In his wheelchair Chapman attended the September 1989 taping for the Monty Python twentieth-anniversary television special. But in early October he was hospitalized after suffering a massive hemorrhage. Graham Chapman died of throat and spinal cancer on October 13, 1989. Some of his last visitors were his old friends and partners, Cleese and Palin. Ironically, in an interview promoting *Jake's Journey* in late 1988 Graham had said, "I really feel now that I'm about to start on my life."

1934-1972

At the end of the 1972 season, Roberto Clemente joined the exclusive 3,000-hit club. But a plane crash three months later robbed him of hit 3001.

Roberto Clemente was one of major league baseball's all-time greats. His .317 lifetime batting average is impressive, as was his daring on the base paths and cannon of an arm in right field. But he is best remembered as the first Latin American baseball superstar. He has become a model for kids, showing them a way to rise above poverty by following the path he blazed to the major leagues.

Roberto was born on August 18, 1934, in Carolina, Puerto Rico. He was the youngest of seven children. His dad, Melchor, was a foreman on a sugarcane plantation, and his mom, Luisa, ran the plantation's grocery store. He had a happy childhood and later said, "My mother and father worked like racehorses for me." Most kids growing up in Puerto Rico play baseball, and Roberto was just like everyone else—an avid fan and a serious player. When he was 17 years old, Roberto was drafted by a Puerto Rican team, the Santurce Cangrejeros (Crabbers). He played three seasons for them. After batting .356 in 1953, he was signed by the Brooklyn Dodgers for a $10,000 bonus. At the time this was the largest bonus ever given to a Latino ballplayer.

The Dodgers assigned Roberto to their Montreal farm team in the International League. Brooklyn managers had so much faith in Roberto's potential that they instructed his manager to use Roberto sparingly so that scouts from other teams would not notice him. In the 1950s one team could draft another team's minor league players. Of his time in Montreal, Roberto later said, "If I struck out, I stayed in the lineup. If I played well I was benched. I didn't know what was going on, and I was confused and almost mad enough to go home."

Despite their precautions, the Dodgers lost Roberto to the Pittsburgh Pirates. The team drafted him in 1954. Given the chance to be the Pirates' everyday right fielder, Clemente responded immediately, batting .255, .311, .253, .289, and .296 in his first five seasons with the team. Roberto was a major factor in Pittsburgh's 1960 World Series championship. That year he hit .314 during the regular season and .310 in the World Series against the New York Yankees. He was disappointed to come in only eighth in the balloting for that year's Most Valuable Player award. Years later he told a reporter, "I was bitter. I still am." The longer he spent in the major leagues, the more vocal Roberto became about the lack of recognition given to Latin- and African-American ballplayers.

Despite his achievements on the field, the press began to portray Roberto as a malingerer. He was injured frequently. His teammate Bill Mazeroski excused Roberto. "When he was hurt he had trouble explaining himself because of the language problem, and everyone thought he was jakin' (malingering). I don't think he ever jaked."

From 1961 to 1965, Roberto consistently batted more than .300. In 1966 he had his career's best records in home runs and RBIs: He hit 29 home runs and batted in 119 runs. That year the nation's sportswriters made up for their past omissions by naming him baseball's Most Valuable Player. Roberto

had another banner year in 1967, leading the National League in batting with a .357 average. When *Sport* magazine polled baseball managers that year, they named Roberto Clemente as the game's top player. One manager said, "He's not only the best today—he's one of the best that's ever played baseball."

After suffering a series of back injuries in 1968 and batting only .291, Roberto briefly considered retiring from baseball. Luckily, he reconsidered. In 1969 he batted .345, only three points behind National League batting champion Pete Rose of the Cincinnati Reds. Clemente hit well despite suffering a shoulder injury.

The Pirates became a major force again in 1970, winning the National League East division with the considerable help of Roberto's .352 average. He had become such a hero in Puerto Rico that when the Pirates held Roberto Clemente Night to honor him about 300,000 Puerto Ricans signed a salutary telegram to him. The following year, the Pirates went all the way, winning the 1971 World Series against the Baltimore Orioles four games to three. Roberto was the hero of the series, batting .414 and hitting two home runs.

Following that season, Roberto Clemente, now 37 years old, seemed to be a changed man. He had largely forgotten earlier slights and misun-

A hard-hitting slugger, Roberto Clemente won four batting titles, compiling a .317 lifetime batting average.

Roberto Clemente, number 21 for the Pittsburgh Pirates, warms up his arm during spring training in 1958.

Before an exhibition game, Roberto Clemente receives one of the many awards for outstanding play that he won during his career in the major leagues.

derstandings from the press. His wounded pride was almost healed. After 17 years in the major leagues, he knew he was a great ballplayer and so did everyone else. Through it all Roberto never forgot his roots. With his wife, Vera, and their three sons, Roberto Jr., Luis, and Enrique, Roberto continued to live in Puerto Rico during the off-season.

At the beginning of the 1970s, Roberto was making just over $100,000 a year. When he demanded a $160,000 salary after the 1971 season, he had more than his own family's benefit in mind. Always proud of his home country, Roberto was very active in Puerto Rican causes. On his own he built a sports city for disadvantaged youth. "They spend millions of dollars for dope control in Puerto Rico," he said. "Why don't they attack it before it starts? You try to get kids so they don't become dope addicts, and it would help to get them interested in sports."

In December 1972 Roberto helped organize relief efforts for victims of a major earthquake in Nicaragua. On December 31 he was aboard a plane carrying supplies bound for Nicaragua when it crashed shortly after takeoff. The 38-year-old superstar, Roberto Clemente, was killed instantly.

Roberto once said, "Anybody who has the opportunity to serve their country or their island and doesn't, God should punish them. If you can be good, why should you be bad?" Puerto Ricans were devastated by the loss of their hero. The inaugural ceremonies for the island's governor were canceled out of respect for Clemente. Just 11 weeks after his death, Roberto Clemente was enshrined in baseball's Hall of Fame—the first Latino player to be so honored.

Today's country women singers owe a lot to Patsy Cline. Before she hit the airwaves, country women were rarely heard on the radio. At concerts women were valued more for their looks than their musical talents. While men had plenty of opportunities to wail about lost romances, broken dreams, and missed opportunities, the women were expected to sing low-key gospel tunes. Then along came Patsy.

She was born Virginia Patterson Hensley on September 8, 1932, in Winchester, Virginia. At the age of four, Patsy won her first talent prize, tap dancing in an amateur contest. By the time she had entered grade school, she was impressing her family with her musical ability. To encourage her talent, Patsy's mother presented her with a new piano on her eighth birthday. Piano lessons helped Patsy learn the basic music patterns. On Sundays she sang with the church choir. By the time she was 14 years old, Patsy was singing regularly on the radio. She got the gig on her own by walking fearlessly into the station and asking for an audition.

When Patsy was 15, her parents divorced, reportedly because of her father's heavy drinking. Without her dad around to pay the bills, music became even more important to Patsy. In the evenings she earned money for her family by singing in clubs. During the day she worked behind the counter at a drugstore. With so much to do, she let her schoolwork slide, and by the end of the year, she officially dropped out.

In 1948 the determined and resourceful Patsy maneuvered herself backstage when Wally Fowler brought his show to her hometown. She persuaded the country gospel singer to listen to her sing. Fowler, who was a regular at the Grand Ole Opry, was sufficiently impressed by her voice to arrange an audition for Patsy with the Opry in Nashville. Confident that she would pass the audition with flying colors, Patsy made plans to settle in Nashville. To her disappointment, the Opry said she was not yet ready for big-time country radio. Despondent, Patsy returned to Winchester, where she continued to hone her talent.

Throughout the early 1950s, Patsy tried to make her mark in the music world. She also fell in love and married Gerald Cline. In 1952 she was the featured vocalist in Bill Peer's Melody Playboys of Brunswick, Maryland. Peer helped Patsy land her first recording contract with 4 Star Records in 1954. She returned to Nashville for the recording sessions, but her early recordings for 4 Star had little effect on her career. Patsy continued to earn her living with live performances, including several appearances at the Opry. In late 1955 Patsy became a regular on *Town and Country Time*, a show hosted by Jimmy Dean in Washington, D.C. She still was not a big star, but she was determined to become one. As often happens to women intent on success, Patsy's fierce determination earned her a reputation for being tough, argumentative, and assertive.

In January 1957 Patsy finally got her big break. She appeared as a contestant on *Arthur Godfrey's Talent Scouts*. For her first network television

1932-1963

Patsy Cline may have sung about one heartache after another, but onstage and off she did not have a victim's personality. She was one tough gal.

Patsy Cline served her apprenticeship as a singer in rough-and-tumble barrooms, where she learned to belt out a tune over the din.

appearance, Patsy selected a torch song that she had recorded a year earlier, "Walkin' After Midnight." When she finished singing, the audience went wild. Patsy won first prize and became a regular on Godfrey's show for the next two weeks. "Walkin' After Midnight" rose quickly on both the country and pop charts. After nine years of struggle, experimentation, and hard work, Patsy Cline had become a star. Unfortunately, her success came with a price she had not anticipated. Patsy's drive and ambition put a tremendous strain on her marriage. Soon after her first appearances on national television, she and Gerald filed for divorce.

In the late 1950s, Patsy briefly shifted her focus away from her career and concentrated on her personal life. She married Charlie Dick, and they soon had two children. Patsy's intense interest in singing could not be kept on a back burner for very long, and when Patsy resumed her career with her usual intensity, her second marriage also felt the strain.

In 1960 Patsy was invited to join the Grand Ole Opry and soon scored her second hit, "I Fall to Pieces." Her record producer, Owen Bradley, took advantage of Patsy's rich voice and backed her with lush string arrangements rather than the twangy sound of a steel guitar, which was heard on

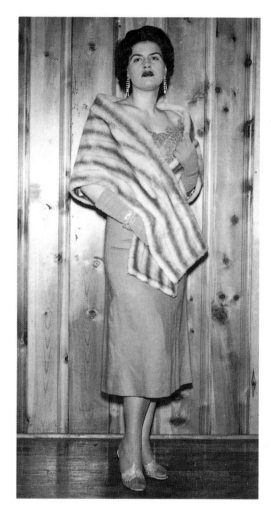

Some country singers are jealous of one another's success, but Patsy, who was fearlessly aggressive about her career, was a good friend to everyone in the business.

Patsy worked hard to achieve success, and she was never ashamed to flaunt what she had whether it was her powerful voice or a new fur stole.

most country-and-western records made at that time. Patsy's sound is a unique blend of emotional hillbilly vocal arrangements and understated pop instrumentation. Her style of music came to be known as the Nashville Sound. Ironically, Cline was not pleased with either "Walkin' After Midnight" or "I Fall to Pieces." Anxious to stay true to her roots, she often expressed a desire to yodel and growl on her records. But she understood that the Nashville Sound was giving her career a major boost and used it during the next two years on several more records, which also become big hits.

On March 5, 1963, Patsy traveled from Nashville to Kansas City, where she appeared in a benefit concert for the family of disc jockey Jack McCall, who had been killed in a traffic accident. Immediately following the performance, she boarded a small plane along with country-Western performers Cowboy Copas and Hawkshaw Hawkins, and Copas's son-in-law Randy Hughes, who piloted the aircraft. Eighty-five miles west of Nashville, the plane encountered some turbulence and crashed. There were no survivors. Shortly before her death, Patsy had been confident that her most recent release, "Sweet Dreams," also would become a hit. It reached number five on the country charts after Patsy Cline died.

1938-1960

A talented guitarist and an energetic performer, Eddie Cochran was one of the first rock musicians to recognize the potential of overdubbing. He performed all the parts on many of his hits.

The first time Eddie Cochran picked up a guitar he was 12 years old. Playfully strumming its strings, the young man felt like he was creating magic. The following Christmas Eddie's parents gave him his first guitar. From then on, mastering his guitar became Eddie's primary focus. When he was not at home practicing, he was at a music store listening to the latest records. Eddie soon became so adept on the guitar that his friends often asked him to play at parties. His music had a particular effect on the young partygoers. It made them want to swerve their hips in rhythm to Eddie's pulsating sounds.

Eddie was born in Oklahoma City on October 3, 1938, and grew up in Minnesota. When Eddie was 14 years old, his family moved to Bell Gardens, California. The kids in Eddie's new neighborhood were intrigued by the sounds they heard coming through his open bedroom window. Word of the new teenager's musical talents quickly spread through the small suburb, and before long Eddie was enjoying his newfound status as a local celebrity.

Songwriter Jerry Capehart was particularly impressed with Eddie when he heard him sing. In 1956 Jerry had formed Ekko records. He recorded Eddie and a friend, Hank Cochran, who was no relation. They called themselves the Cochran Brothers, and their records were not big hits.

At this time Elvis Presley was taking the country by storm with his soulful singing and gyrating hips. Si Waronker, an executive at Liberty records, heard Eddie's music and thought he might be able to make Eddie into Liberty's answer to Elvis. Waronker arranged a meeting with Eddie to discuss his recording solo for Liberty. Since Hank had already left California for Nashville, where he planned to write and record his own material, Eddie decided the timing was right and hoped that Liberty had the know-how to deliver what he wanted most—a hit record.

To launch Eddie's solo career, Liberty records arranged for him to make a brief appearance in a feature film, *The Girl Can't Help It*, starring Jayné Mansfield. Eddie sang "Twenty Flight Rock." Liberty intended to release the song as Eddie's first single but substituted "Sittin' in the Balcony." The record shot to number 18 on the charts, but Eddie was determined to succeed with his own identity. He turned to his buddy Jerry Capehart for help. In the spring of 1958, they collaborated on "Summertime Blues," experimenting with different arrangements for the song until they hit upon what would become known as Eddie's signature sound, a combination of acoustic guitars, hand clapping, and a hard driving beat. "Summertime Blues" scored big with teenage listeners and quickly became one of Liberty's biggest successes. Suddenly, the label was no longer interested in making Eddie sound like Elvis.

In 1959 Eddie met Sharon Sheeley, who had written Ricky Nelson's hit "Poor Little Fool." The couple exchanged opinions about various groups and discovered that their tastes were similar. Eddie asked Sharon if she would write

The stance, the clothes, and the slicked-back hair were de rigueur for a teen idol, but Eddie Cochran's considerable musical talent made him more than just another cool kid with a guitar.

Eddie's unique style and the way he tuned his Gretsch semi-acoustic guitar changed the direction of rock music, especially in England, where he was a major influence on Peter Townshend as well as many New Wave guitarists.

a song with him. Their collaboration produced "Somethin' Else," which Liberty released in September 1959.

In early 1960 Eddie toured England for 10 weeks. Recognizing that the road could be lonely, he invited Sharon to join him. The tour closed with a week's engagement in London. The next day, Eddie and Sharon were scheduled to return to the States on an early-morning flight. During the chauffeur-driven ride to the airport, Eddie and Sharon enthusiastically exchanged ideas about the new songs they wanted to write together. On a lonely stretch of road near Chippenham, Wiltshire, one of the tires suddenly blew out. The driver tried to steer the swerving car off the road and out of the way of an oncoming vehicle, but he collided with the other car. Sharon's back was permanently injured. Eddie Cochran sustained severe head injuries and died several hours later on April 17, 1960.

1919-1965

Nat "King" Cole's unique voice
could transform the most
ordinary tune into a masterful
jazz number

In the 1940s the line between black music and white music was clearly drawn. Nat "King" Cole crossed that line with a soft, sure step that opened the way for other musicians, including his own daughters Carol and Natalie. Cole faced down prejudice without flamboyance, relying on his incredible integrity to see him through every crisis.

Nathaniel Adams Coles, the youngest son of Rev. Edward and Perlina Coles, was born in Montgomery, Alabama on March 17, 1919. His family soon moved to Chicago, and along with his brothers, Nat received his first musical training at the True Light Baptist Church, where Edward was the pastor and Perlina was the choir director. Before he ever took a music class in school, Nat could improvise jazz tunes on the piano. With some formal training, he had become the church's organist by the time he was 12.

While he was still in high school, Nat put together his first band. When he was 17 years old, Nat got his first professional gig as the arranger and conductor of a road show called *Shuffle Along*. During the tour he married one of the chorus girls, Nadine Robinson. When the show disbanded in Los Angeles, the young couple put down roots and began performing in local clubs. Nat soon got a trio together with Oscar Moore on guitar and Wesley Prince on bass. He dropped the *S* from his last name and was dubbed the King by a nightclub manager who asked Cole to wear a gold paper crown as a promotional gimmick.

In the late 1930s, the group was playing the hottest New York and Hollywood nightclubs. Shy and insecure about his quiet singing voice, it never occurred to Nat to step in front of the microphone as a vocalist until his trio almost lost a club date because it did not have a singer. Reluctantly, he accepted the advice of his friend, veteran composer Phil Moore, and began to sing.

Capitol records decided to risk promoting a middle-of-the-road black artist and released Cole's classic "Straighten Up and Fly Right." (Nat claimed that one of his dad's sermons inspired the song's lyrics.) Capitol's risk paid off with a half million sales in 1943 and 1944. On later releases he strayed further from his jazz roots, and soon Cole was appearing with full-sized orchestras, sometimes with the trio and other times solo. In 1946 the King Cole Trio replaced Bing Crosby on the Kraft Music Hall Show. Nat became the first African-American musician to host his own network radio program.

This suave, easygoing performer was plagued with controversy he did not create and could not control. The press criticized his style because it made "white girls swoon," but other black musicians thought that Cole didn't have enough soul. In 1948 he and his second wife, Marie Ellington, bought a home in the fashionable Hancock Park suburb of Los Angeles. Homeowners protested the sale of the property to an African American, but the Supreme Court defended his right to own the home.

The King Cole Trio, with Wesley Prince on bass, Oscar Moore on guitar, and Nat on piano, was joined by a drummer in the early 1950s.

The versatile performer made four major movies: *Breakfast in Holly-wood* (1946), *China Gate* (1957), *St. Louis Blues* (1958), and *Cat Ballou* (1965). But with the advent of rock 'n' roll, Cole sold fewer records. His recording company asked him to change his style, but Cole steadfastly refused. Even though his record sales were off, Nat was always popular on tour. He made several sweeps through Europe, played Carnegie Hall, and was a frequent guest on television variety shows. In 1956 he got a show of his own and used it to present other African-American musicians to the television audience. Unfortunately, the American public wasn't ready to hear what Cole had to offer, and the series was cancelled in 1957. During the season the show aired, Cole was attacked onstage during a concert by six men.

Nat's self-assurance and belief in his music never wavered, but his health did. On February 15, 1965, he lost his struggle with lung cancer. His music lives on. Twenty-five years after his death, Christmas would not be Christmas without Nat "King" Cole singing "The Christmas Song."

1926-1967

In 1964, when this photograph was taken, John Coltrane recorded *A Love Supreme*, a four-movement suite expressing Trane's feeling that music is a form of meditation or prayer.

In the annals of jazz, only a handful of musicians are recognized worldwide by their nicknames alone. There is Duke (Duke Ellington), Pres (Lester Young), and Bird (Charlie Parker). Then there is Trane—John Coltrane. Just as Parker's advanced playing set the jazz world on its ear in the late 1940s, Coltrane's further progressions on the saxophone kept things hopping in the 1950s and 1960s.

Coltrane was born in Hamlet, North Carolina, on September 23, 1926. His father was a tailor and amateur musician, who died when John was 12. While he was growing up, the serious young man usually had his nose in a book, but at night John was entranced by the sounds of jazz on the radio. He started to play clarinet in elementary school, but switched to alto saxophone in high school. John continued studying music after graduation, when he and two buddies moved to Philadelphia. The move also put him closer to his mother, Alice, who had gone to live in Atlantic City in search of a better job. John was drafted into the Navy in 1945 and assigned to play in dance and marching bands in Hawaii.

After the service John signed up for music school, but he soon joined a touring band. He played with many of the great dance bands, including those led by Eddie "Cleanhead" Vinson, Dizzy Gillespie, Earl Bostic, and Johnny Hodges. By the late 1940s, Coltrane had an obvious weight problem, he began drinking heavily, and like many jazz men of his time, he became addicted to heroin.

Despite his addiction, 1955 was an important year for John. He married his first wife, Naima, and began to make a national reputation for himself playing and recording with trumpeter Miles Davis. Now living in New York, John began to record for the Prestige and Blue Note record labels. In 1957 he quit heroin and alcohol cold turkey. That same year he said he experienced a spiritual awakening and returned to the study of Eastern religions, philosophies, and music that he had begun in the early 1950s.

One critic writing in 1958 described John's harmonically complex style as "sheets of sound." But not everyone found the dense texture of his music appealing. The critics remained evenly split on John Coltrane: Some people felt he was a musical genius; others labeled his music antijazz. Debates between critics aside, Coltrane had a fanatical following. When one fan played back one of his solos on a 50-cent kazoo, Trane was so touched that he treated the man to dinner. For another fan who arrived at a club just as Coltrane was walking off the bandstand, John returned to play him a 15-minute unaccompanied version of "My Favorite Things." His home became a refuge for young musicians, who idolized him for both his music and his quiet, generous manner. One college jazz teacher compared the impact of Coltrane's music on other musicians with Bach and Brahms.

Soon after forming the John Coltrane Quartet, John signed with Impulse Records. His music remained controversial. When *A Love Supreme* was

After Trane cleaned up his life in the late 1950s, he became a serious student of music theory. Instead of relaxing with the band, he often continued to practice between sets at clubs.

Trane taped his last record at the studios of the Village Vanguard. This photograph may have been taken at that recording session.

released *Down Beat* magazine assigned two writers to review it. One critic awarded the LP five stars; the other gave it only one.

Divorced from Naima and married to Alice McLeod, a jazz pianist, John Coltrane had three sons in quick succession. John's fame spread worldwide. Landing at Tokyo's airport for a tour of Japan in 1966, he was amazed to find a crowd of several thousand fans to greet him. His music grew more adventurous each year, taking in Indian and African influences.

In 1967 John's health began to fail; he was beset by headaches and stomach problems. Rushed to a Long Island hospital in excruciating pain, he died the next day, July 11, 1967, from the effects of liver cancer. A memorial service in New York a few days later attracted hundreds of friends and fans. At age 40, the mighty Trane had run out of steam.

1931-1964

At home in the recording studio
and onstage, Sam Cooke was
a talented musician who
translated the gospel music he
sang as a child into bluesy
ballads that climbed the charts.

His gospel roots were deep, but Sam Cooke grafted them to secular themes and came up with the first successful sounds of soul music. Sam's life-long love of gospel music was totally authentic. He was the son of a Baptist minister, born on January 2, 1931, in Clarksdale, Mississippi. Along with his seven brothers and sisters, he grew up in Chicago singing in the choir at his father's church. When he was only nine years old, Sam organized the Singing Children, a music group that included one of his brothers and two of his sisters. The group sang at churches in his neighborhood.

Sam was always a good kid and a fine student, and he was deeply committed to his religion. After graduating from high school, he sang for a short time with the Highway QC's, a gospel group. The quartet had heard about Sam, but they had never heard him. Until one day, when the group was walking past Sam's house, they heard him practicing. They knocked on his door and hired him on the spot.

Since he had been singing in churches for most of his life, Sam jumped at the chance to join the Soul Stirrers as their lead vocalist. The Soul Stirrers were a popular gospel group that had been singing together since the 1930s. Nineteen-year-old Sam was thrilled to replace the retiring star R.H. Harris and was soon in the groove of touring the country and performing for large audiences.

During a gig at the Los Angeles Shrine Auditorium in 1957, a record company executive noticed Sam's sweet, clear voice and asked him to record a single. Sam was no novice in the recording studio. He had already recorded several gospel hits with the Soul Stirrers. But he was nervous about recording a secular song and wanted the Soul Stirrers to know nothing about the record. Sam recorded the single under the name Dale Cook, but despite his precautions, the Soul Stirrers found out that Sam had ventured out on his own. They immediately found themselves a new lead singer, and Sam was out of a job.

Sam's single went nowhere. He was distraught but not because his song flopped. He felt disloyal to gospel music. Producer Bumps Blackwell spent months attempting to sway Sam to give secular music one more try. Desperate and still out of work, Cooke finally relented and recorded a tune he coauthored with his brother L.C. called "You Send Me." It sold two and a half million copies for Keen Records.

Sam Cooke's suave good looks
coupled with his pure, clear
voice were the original image
and sound of soul.

The label only wanted to turn Sam into a black teen idol, but his talent far exceeded their expectations. Recording for Keen, Sam had hits with all kinds of music, including "Everybody Likes to Cha Cha Cha" (1959), "Only Sixteen" (1959), and "Wonderful World" (1960). Cooke switched to a major label, RCA Records, in 1960. He and Harry Belafonte were RCA's only black recording stars, and the company had definite plans for the young performer. He was encouraged to add a harder edge to his music and to be as soulful as he wanted to be. Sam had been pushing for this direction because he still felt guilty about moving away from his gospel roots. The swift rise of "Chain Gang" to the number two spot on the charts let Sam and RCA know that the world really was ready for soul.

Sam's career shifted into high gear. He appeared frequently on network television and played to capacity audiences in large arenas throughout the country. He also became one of the first successful African-American record company executives, organizing his own company, Sar/Derby, to develop black recording artists. While Sam continued to record for RCA, he was producing "Lookin' for a Love" by Bobby Womack and the Valentinos and "When a Boy Falls in Love" by Mel Carter. He also gave such artists as Johnnie Taylor and Billy Preston their first recording contracts.

Sam's luck seemed to have run out in 1963. He was almost blinded in a car accident that killed a close friend. Then his infant son drowned in a freak accident. But worse was yet to come. No one could have predicted the events that took place on December 11, 1964. Despite his being a major star and constantly under the watchful eye of the press, Sam maintained his untarnished image as a clean-cut good kid, who had remained loyal to his religious roots. Everyone's belief that Sam Cooke was practically a saint made the events of that terrible night especially shocking. Even today it seems impossible that what happened could actually have happened.

The pieced-together story goes something like this: Sam met a 22-year-old woman at a party. She says that he forced her to ride with him to a Los Angeles motel. While Sam was in the bathroom, the young woman ran off with his clothes. Clad in only a sports shirt and shoes, Sam ran out of the room after her. He began pounding on the door of the motel's manager, who says he went berserk and broke the door open. The manager and Sam scuffled. She grabbed her pistol and shot Sam Cooke three times. Unsure that he was dead, she then beat the mortally wounded singer with club. A coroner's jury ruled that the motel manager's actions were justifiable homicide. Sam had not yet celebrated his thirtieth birthday.

Following his death, RCA released "A Change Is Gonna Come." The song was briefly top 40, but fans were too shocked by the sordid details of Sam's death to make it a hit. The sweet soul sound that Sam Cooke made famous lives on in the music of many popular performers: The Animals, Aretha Franklin, Dr. Hook, Otis Redding, Rod Stewart, and Cat Stevens to name but a few of the artists who have recorded his work.

When Sam Cooke stepped in front of an audience, he was always suave and sophisticated.

Singer-songwriter Jim Croce's public life was brief, but his star burned brightly. His direct style and genius for writing both story songs and sensitive ballads keep his name and his music alive.

Jim was born on January 10, 1943, in a working-class section of Philadelphia. His Italian-American family wanted him to learn to play the accordion, but he was 18 before he got serious about playing music. Putting aside the accordion, he bought a 12-string acoustic guitar and taught himself to play it.

After a short stint in the Army, where he met the character who inspired "Bad, Bad Leroy Brown," Jim enrolled at Villanova University in his hometown. He worked on a degree in psychology, but he also spent a lot of time playing music, performing solo gigs and working with bands. "While everyone in my senior class was going out on job interviews," he said, "all I wanted to do was play my guitar." After graduation Jim ended up working in construction. On the job he broke one of his fingers with a sledgehammer. Playing the guitar was so important to Jim that he practiced for long hours so he could pick without using the damaged finger. In 1966 Jim married his girlfriend Ingrid. She was also a singer. The following fall Jim began teaching at a junior high school in South Philadelphia, but he still felt that he wanted to be a singer.

In 1967 Jim and Ingrid moved to New York to try their luck as a folk duo in the city's clubs and coffeehouses. Capitol Records signed them to a recording contract and released their spectacularly unsuccessful album, *Jim and Ingrid Croce.* Today, it is a treasured collector's item. Feeling like total failures and ready to give up on the music business, the couple returned to the Philadelphia area. They lived in a farmhouse, and Jim took odd jobs to pay the rent. With a baby on the way, the couple's financial situation grew so bad that Jim was forced to pawn his guitars to pay their bills. When their son, Adrian, was born in 1970, Jim got a job driving a truck. At the time it seemed like the perfect job for Jim because he could compose songs in his head while he was on the road.

One of Jim's old college buddies, Tommy West, was part of a successful New York singing duo, Cashman and West. He encouraged Jim to record some of his newer songs and again start courting the record companies. In 1971 Jim recorded some songs with his new musical partner Maury Muehleisen on second guitar. (Maury later accompanied him on all his greatest hits.) The following year, ABC Records signed Jim and released *You Don't Mess Around with Jim.* The title song and "Operator" both became top 20 hits.

After years of struggling, Jim Croce suddenly could do no wrong. Within in a short time, he was a regular on television and performed in more than 250 concerts a year. His 1973 album, *Life and Times,* included his first number one hit "Bad, Bad Leroy Brown." Jim always wrote about the kind of people he met in bars and when he was working construction.

1943-1973

Jim Croce was not an overnight sensation. He spent many years working construction and driving a truck before his musical genius was recognized.

Within a few months after Jim's death, three of his LPs were in the top 20: *I've Got a Name* and *You Don't Mess Around with Jim* were both number one, while *Life and Times* was number seven.

He claimed that if he had to go back to driving a truck or a bulldozer, it would not make much difference to him.

On September 20, 1973, Jim and Maury boarded a private plane in Natchitoches, Louisiana. They were on their way to a gig in Texas. The plane crashed during takeoff, killing everyone on board. Jim Croce was dead at 30, but his hits continued. "I've Got a Name," "Time in a Bottle," and "I'll Have to Say I Love You in a Song" were posthumous releases. In the lyrics to the wistful "Time in a Bottle," Jim left his own best epitaph: "There never seems to be enough time to do the things you want to do."

Bobby Darin's ambition was to become a legend by the time he was 25, and he did. He was born Walden Robert Cassotto on May 14, 1936. (Darin found his stage name on the broken neon sign of a Mandarin restaurant.) Growing up in a tough section of the Bronx, he barely survived several serious bouts with rheumatic fever and learned to think of life as a fight he wanted to win. He taught himself to play drums, piano, and guitar. In his late teens, Bobby met fledgling publisher Don Kirshner in a candy store. The two collaborated on commercial jingles. Kirshner helped arrange a trial run at Atco records. In 1958, after several forgettable recordings, Bobby came up with a big winner, a song called "Splish Splash" that he had spent 20 minutes writing. Darin's biggest single success, "Mack the Knife," climbed the charts the following year.

Wanting it all, Bobby went to Hollywood in 1960, where he starred with his future wife, Sandra Dee, in *Come September* and received an Oscar nomination for *Captain Newman, M.D.* As rock 'n' roll swept the nation, Bobby scaled down his career. He performed in clubs and on college campuses, as well as in Las Vegas. His recording of Tim Hardin's "If I Were a Carpenter" was number eight on the pop charts in 1966.

Bobby worked tirelessly for Robert Kennedy's presidential campaign. After Kennedy was killed in Los Angeles, Darin retreated from the entertainment world. He sold his possessions and lived in seclusion in a mobile home in Big Sur. After a year away from the music business, Bobby started his own company, Direction Records, and brought out an album, *Born Walden Robert Cassotto*.

He married for a second time and returned to the Vegas stage. At his last performances, Darin was less driven than he had been. He did not have to work to win over the crowds; he knew they were his fans before he even walked onstage. He usually made his entrance to a standing ovation. Now, he truly was a legend.

In December 1973 Bobby checked in to Cedars of Lebanon Hospital for open-heart surgery. After six hours on the operating table, he finally lost the fight.

1936-1973

In 1958, when this photograph was made, Bobby Darin scored his first big hits with "Splish Splash" and "Queen of the Hop."

1931-1955

This picture of James Dean was taken when he was four years old and living in Indiana with his parents.

James Dean was born on February 8, 1931, in Marion, Indiana. He was the only child of Winton Dean, a dental technician, and Mildred Wilson Dean, a farm wife. When James was five years old, his family moved to Santa Monica, California. Four years later, Mildred died suddenly from cancer. Winton decided to stay on in California, but he sent James back to Indiana, where he was raised by his aunt Hortense and his uncle Marcus Winslow on their small farm in Fairmount.

Hortense and Marcus decided that the best way for them to help James recover from his loss was to offer the boy an all-American childhood. They enrolled him in 4-H Club and encouraged his artistic nature with dance classes and drawing lessons. When James was 11 years old, Marcus taught him how to use a BB gun. On his next birthday, his aunt and uncle gave him a motorbike. By the time James reached high school, he was actively involved in sports. Despite his being only five feet seven inches tall, he was accepted on the basketball team. He also ran track. But his favorite activity was drama. The school's drama teacher, Adeline Nall, was particularly impressed by James's talent and encouraged him to audition for productions. In his senior year, James competed in a statewide dramatic speaking event. His highly charged performance included yelling and a physical collapse onstage. To Adeline Nall's delight, he came in first place. Several months later he repeated his performance in a nationwide contest but lost on a technicality: He would not cut his 12-minute speech to fit the allotted 10 minutes.

Following his high school graduation, James hoped to study theatre in college. But his father, who had kept in steady contact with James from California, convinced him that his idea was impractical. Winton encouraged his son to study law. In the summer of 1949, James moved in with Winton and his new wife in Santa Monica. That fall James enrolled in a prelaw program at Santa Monica City College. The many years that they had been separated contributed to an uneasy relationship between father and son. They bickered constantly. Winton was especially peeved when James transferred to UCLA in his sophomore year. He understood that James was attracted to the school because of its nationally renowned theatre department, but he felt his son was making a mistake. The situation worsened when James was cast in his first play at UCLA. He played Malcolm in Macbeth. Although James received only mediocre notices for his performance, a talent agent who had seen the

On location for *Rebel Without a Cause*, Jimmy relaxes with a cigarette between takes.

Natalie Wood seeks to inspire Jimmy's courage before the chicken run in *Rebel Without a Cause*.

production was impressed and signed James as a client. A few weeks later, James landed his first professional job, appearing in a Pepsi-Cola commercial.

Realizing life with his father was never going to be easy, James left home and moved on campus. But the rowdiness of campus life turned him off, and a few months later, he was sharing a small apartment with a fellow theatre arts major, William Bast. Determined to succeed as a professional actor, James often cut classes to audition. He supported himself working as a parking-lot attendant. In the spring of 1951, he was cast in his first dramatic television role as John the Baptist in *Hill Number One*. A group of high school girls who had seen the program were so smitten by James that they formed his first fan club.

In the summer of 1951, James met Rogers Brackett, an account supervisor and television director. Impressed with Dean, Brackett became his mentor and recommended the younger man to his friends for parts in their television productions. A few months later, James moved in with Brackett.

Bored and frustrated with the small roles he was attracting in Hollywood, James moved to New York, where he hoped to work exclusively in theatre. To pay the rent, he used his connection with Brackett to land a job rehearsing contestants for the game show *Beat the Clock*. Occasionally, he also appeared in minor parts on such live television shows as *Studio One* and *Kraft Theater*. James's acting style moved in a completely new direction when he became a member of the Actors Studio, which was headed by Lee Strasberg, who also taught such talented students as Marilyn Monroe, Marlon Brando, and Shelley Winters.

Once James became a member of the Actors Studio, it was the only thing that remained a constant in his life while he was living in New York. He was always changing apartments; either staying with friends or sharing Brackett's studio when he was in town. He dated frequently and established a particularly close romantic relationship with Elizabeth Sheridan, a struggling dancer.

In October 1952 Brackett introduced James to Lemuel Ayers, who was preparing to produce Richard Nash's play *See the Jaguar*. The introduction led to James's winning the lead role. Unfortunately, the play opened and closed within a week. But Walter Kerr, a highly respected and influential critic, saw the show and hailed Dean's performance as extraordinary. This caused several producers and casting directors suddenly to take notice of the young actor. A string of roles in television dramas soon followed.

Even though his career had begun to take off, James was developing a reputation for being difficult. He arrived at rehearsals late, quarreled with directors over stage notes, missed cues, and frequently fell asleep. Dennis Stock, a photographer who was Dean's friend, recalled, "Jimmy was an insomniac—so at odd times and in odd places he would simply pass out, for a few minutes or a few hours, then wake up and set out again. He lived like a stray animal; in fact, come to think of it, he was a stray animal."

In November 1954 Dean was cast as Bachir, the homosexual Arab houseboy in Andre Gide's *The Immoralist*. Geraldine Page and Louis Jourdan received star billing. Ruth Goetz, who also appeared in the production, did not enjoy working with Dean: "The little son of a bitch was one of the most unspeakably detestable fellows to work with I ever knew in my life." Despite the unfavorable notices he received from his costars, Dean's performance in *The Immoralist* won him the Daniel Blum Theater Award that season as "the best newcomer of the year." Dean celebrated by buying himself a motorcycle. Shelley Winters, who first met Dean while they were studying together at the Actors Studio, recalled that he was a reckless driver who pulled unnecessary and dangerous stunts when he was behind the wheel.

Midway through the production's run, Dean gave the required three-week notice. He was returning to Hollywood to star in his first motion picture, *East of Eden*. Elia Kazan, the movie's director, was aware of the dangerous stunts Dean pulled and forbade him to drive his motorcycle while the film was being shot. To keep a close eye on Dean, Kazan assigned him a lavish dressing room on the lot next door to his office. Years later, Kazan told a reporter that he had never thought Dean was anything more than a limited actor who could work hard and that he was a very neurotic young man. He was perfect for the part of the boy in *East of Eden*, Kazan said, but even at that time the director felt that he was deeply troubled and that later Dean just got worse.

In *Rebel Without a Cause*, the three teenagers, Sal Mineo, James Dean, and Natalie Wood, form a family outside the control of adult authority.

Just two weeks before he died, at about the time this photo was taken, Jimmy made a 30-second commercial for the National Highway Committee in which he warned everyone to drive safely "because the life you save may be . . . mine."

Jimmy would avail himself of any opportunity to wear a costume. For this publicity shot, he adopted a Wild West look.

During the filming Dean became romantically involved with starlet Pier Angeli. Dozens of stories cropped up in fan magazines promising "intimate" details about their relationship. The affair ended suddenly after a few months, when Pier gave in to pressure from her disapproving family. A short while later, she married pop singer Vic Damone. Dean pretended not to care, but his close friends could see that he was hurt by the news of their wedding.

The world premiere of *East of Eden* was held in New York City on March 10, 1955. Dean chose to stay in Hollywood and missed out on the festivities. The critics hailed him as "the screen's most sensational male find of the year." His off-screen activities also entertained the press, and reporters had a field day writing about his often self-destructive exploits. Ezra Goodman, a reporter for *Life* magazine, wrote about Dean's impossible behavior in restaurants, reporting that if he thought he was not getting enough attention, "he would beat a tom-tom solo on the tabletop, play his spoon against a water glass with a boogie beat, pour a bowl of sugar into his pocket, or set fire to a paper napkin."

By the time *Variety* listed *East of Eden* as the country's top-grossing film, Warner Bros. had already signed Dean to a new contract. He was to star in nine films over a six-year period with a minimum salary of $15,000 per picture. Dean's first big purchase upon signing of the contract was a $4,000 Porsche Speedster, which he immediately entered in a race in Palm Springs. Dean had never before driven a race car in competition, but he won the

Dean's riveting performance in *East of Eden* caused the movie to become an internationally popular film.

On the set of the movie *Giant*, Jimmy practices his rope tricks.

amateur class. He also placed third in the professional class. Winning a car race was exactly the kind of encouragement James did not need. A reporter who questioned him about his potentially dangerous new hobby received this response: "Racing is the only time I feel whole."

On March 28, 1955, the cameras rolled on Dean's next movie, *Rebel Without a Cause*, directed by Nicholas Ray and costarring Natalie Wood and Sal Mineo. Dean was cast as Jim Stark, a rebellious teenager. His character had an unhappy relationship with his parents, and he also had trouble fitting in with his classmates at his new high school. As soon as *Rebel* had finished shooting, Dean started work on his third starring role as Jeff Rink in *Giant*, directed by George Stevens and costarring Elizabeth Taylor and Rock Hudson. Dean's role, in which he ages from 25 to approximately 45 by the story's end, challenged the actor to stretch his talents to the maximum. Like Kazan, Stevens forbade Dean to drive during the time the movie was being shot. Stevens even took the extreme step of having the studio confiscate the car it had lent to Dean. The principal shooting for *Giant* was completed in September 1955. With two movies waiting to be released, Dean's career was moving at a smooth pace, but he was anxious to return to his favorite pastime, race-car driving.

On September 30, 1955, Dean and his mechanic Rolf Wuertherich headed to Salinas for a race. Several weeks earlier Dean had traded in his Speedster for a new Porsche Spyder, and he was anxious to see how it performed on the open road. During the long drive, he was stopped by a traffic officer and given a ticket for driving 65 MPH in a 45-MPH zone. Unfortunately, the ticket did not deter James Dean from speeding. Shortly before 5:45 P.M., he was once again speeding. Dean was on a narrow strip of roadway when he lost control of his car and crashed into an oncoming car. James Dean was killed on impact. He was 24 years old. The posthumous releases of *Giant* and *Rebel Without a Cause* have guaranteed that Dean will forever remain a romantic symbol of youth.

1945-1988

Harris Glenn Milstead dressed somewhat conservatively when he was not in character as Divine. Director John Waters said recently that he had always wanted to produce the musical *Oklahoma* with Milstead cast in all the parts.

Mother and daughter, Divine and Ricki Lane, challenge their archrivals at the television studio in this scene from *Hairspray*.

Movie actor Harris Glenn Milstead, better known as Divine, happily epitomized bad taste. Divine was the outrageous 300-pound star of several of director John Waters's low-budget, comically shocking movies, including *Pink Flamingos*, *Female Trouble*, and *Polyester*. The two men grew up together in Baltimore, where neither was ever considered to be just an ordinary kid. Milstead, who was born on October 19, 1945, became notorious in high school. He felt that he could not play sports and was forced to take girls' gym. His fellow students taunted Milstead, and eventually, a police car was assigned to escort him to school every morning. Waters felt an immediate rapport with his overweight classmate and struck up a friendship. They often fantasized about making movies together. In 1966, when Waters directed his second film, *Roman Candles*, he tapped Divine to be his star.

Although Milstead frequently played women's roles, he took exception with being called a female impersonator. "I don't do Judy Garland or Mae West," he told a reporter in 1976. "I'm an actor." Theater audiences enjoyed his performances in *Women Behind Bars* and *The Neon Woman*. In 1986 critics praised his performance as a man in Alan Rudolph's movie *Trouble in Mind*. In early 1988 Milstead played two roles in Waters's first mainstream hit, *Hairspray*. His performances as both a tawdry housewife and a bigoted television-station owner were singled out by critics.

In March 1988 Milstead traveled to Los Angeles to guest star in an episode of *Married . . . with Children*. During a break from rehearsals, he said he was tired and returned to his hotel, where he planned to rest. Several hours later, Milstead was found dead, the apparent victim of heart failure. He was 42 years old.

Tab Hunter, who costarred with Divine in *Polyester* and *Lust in the Dust*, described him as being "like Annette Funicello gone bananas in a pasta factory. Outside of his drag, he was a wonderful, kind, lovely human being."

The defense attorney argued that it was a crime of passion. The judge who heard the trial disagreed. He ruled, "It was a case, pure and simple, of murder, murder with malice." On October 30, 1982, 26-year-old John Thomas Sweeney, arrived at the home of his former girlfriend, 22-year-old actress Dominique Dunne, to attempt a reconciliation. Several weeks earlier, following a violent quarrel, she had demanded that Sweeney move out of the house they had shared. When Dominique refused to reconcile with him, Sweeney became angry and started strangling her. A short while later, police arrived to find Dominique unconscious in the driveway. Sweeney, who worked as a chef at Ma Maison, a trendy Los Angeles restaurant, allegedly told an officer, "I killed my girlfriend." Dominique was rushed to Cedars-Sinai Hospital, where she died six days later. The cause of her death was strangulation.

Dominique Dunne was the daughter of Dominick Dunne, who was a television and movie producer while his daughter was growing up but is now a best-selling novelist and a regular contributor to *Vanity Fair* magazine. Her uncle, John Gregory Dunne, was also a noted writer. Her brother, Griffin Dunne, is a Hollywood movie producer and actor.

Dominique was on her way to becoming a successful movie actress when she was murdered. Her best-known role was Dana Freeling, the oldest daughter in *Poltergeist*, which was released in 1982. Steven Spielberg cowrote and coproduced the movie. Dominique also guest starred on several television shows including, *Family Ties*, *Fame*, and *Lou Grant*.

Immediately following Dominique's death, John Sweeney was charged with murder and assault. Several weeks later, after hearing a detective testify that he had admitted choking Dunne, Sweeney attempted suicide by slashing his wrists with a disposable razor. A year later, he was convicted of strangling Dunne and sentenced to six years in prison. Dominique's grieving father and her many friends were outraged by his light sentence.

Coincidentally, Heather O'Rourke, who played Dominique's little sister in *Poltergeist,* is buried not far from Dunne's grave in a Los Angeles cemetery. She died of a gastrointestinal problem at the age of 13, just six years after Dominique.

1960-1982

Dominique Dunne was an up-and-coming young star when her life ended in tragedy.

Dominique (far right) and other members of the Freeling family await the next terrible thing that will befall them in the 1982 movie *Poltergeist.*

1941-1974

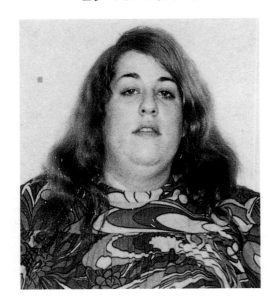

Cass Elliot hoped to free herself from the flower-power image she joyfully embraced in the mid 1960s and become known as a ballad singer.

The life of singer and actress Cass Elliot is a perfect example of talent and sheer force of will overcoming physical shortcomings. Her burnished contralto vocals with the Mamas and the Papas and her self-directed sense of humor made Mama Cass a much-loved star of pop culture in the 1960s and 1970s.

Cass Elliot was born Ellen Naomi Cohen in Baltimore, Maryland, on September 19, 1941. When she was 19 years old, she moved to New York City, where she changed her name to Cass Elliot. By the early 1960s, Cass had made herself a home in the Greenwich Village folk-music scene. She sang with a group called the Mugwumps, which also included future Lovin' Spoonful members John Sebastian and Zal Yanovsky. Another member of the group was singer Denny Doherty. He and Cass created the Mamas and the Papas along with John and Michelle Phillips.

After struggling in New York for a few years, the group moved to Los Angeles, where their glorious four-part harmonies and bohemian look immediately caused a stir. Signed to ABC-Dunhill Records, the Mamas and the Papas exploded across the radio airwaves in 1966, chalking up four top 10 hits: "California Dreaming," "Monday Monday," "I Saw Her Again," and "Words of Love." Mama Cass sang the lead on "Words of Love." The Mamas and the Papas never repeated their 1966 success, but they had two more hits the following year, "Dedicated to the One I Love" and the autobiographical "Creeque Alley," with its famous line, "And no one is getting fat except for Mama Cass."

John, who wrote most of their songs, was the group's musical leader, but Cass was their spiritual leader. She was always the earth mother, weighing more than 200 pounds and usually clad in a tentlike muumuu. "I feel hipbones are overrated," she once said, with typical humor. Cass's house in bucolic Laurel Canyon near Los Angeles became a popular place for pop stars to hang out. Although she was never considered to be even remotely beautiful, her friends were enchanted by her inner beauty. Graham Nash remembers his first encounter with Cass at a Mamas and Papas recording session. "I wanted to check out Michelle Phillips, the beautiful one," he said. "But I totally fell for Cass. Her sense of humor and her mind floored me." Cass ended up playing a significant role in creating the group Crosby, Stills, and Nash, when she introduced Graham to her friends David Crosby and Stephen Stills.

When the Mamas and the Papas split up in 1968, Cass struck out on her own. Switching from rock to ballads, she had her biggest hit with "Dream a Little Dream of Me" in 1968. She was a regular on television talk and variety shows, and hosted her own special in 1969. The show was called "Don't Call Me Mama Anymore." She recorded a poorly received duet album with British singer-songwriter Dave Mason in 1971, and then turned her full energies toward acting. She was a fantastically evil Witch Hazel in the movie version of the television series *Pufnstuf*.

During the mid 1970s, Cass seemed content with her life. She gave birth to a daughter, Owen Vanessa, but even her best friends had no clues to the identity of her little girl's father. While Cass was in London for two concerts at the Palladium, she died in her hotel room on July 29, 1974. She had choked to death on the sandwich she was eating when she suffered a heart attack. Cass Elliot was 32 years old. Michelle Phillips had talked to Cass by phone the night before she died. Michelle remembers that Cass was elated by the standing ovations that she received after both shows. "To her it was the ultimate success, to have done it on her own," said Michelle. "I know that when she died she felt that she'd made the jump from Mama Cass to Cass Elliot."

The Mamas and the Papas in 1966 were, from left to right, Denny Doherty, Mama Cass, Michelle Phillips, and John Phillips.

1940-1986

Perry Ellis helped begin an
enduring trend toward
comfortable, classic clothes.

Perry Ellis was born in Portsmouth, Virginia, in 1940. Until he was nine years old, his family lived with his grandmother in her huge old house that was filled with vintage clothing, which had belonged to Perry's aunts. Ellis, who was an only child, spent many afternoons rummaging through closets and trunks, marvelling at the clothes. In the evening, before bedtime, he leafed through his mother's copies of *Vogue* magazine.

Following graduation from high school, Perry majored in business at the College of William and Mary in Williamsburg, Virginia. Later, he attended New York University, where he earned a master's degree in retailing. In 1963 Perry returned to Virginia to begin his first job as a sportswear buyer for Miller & Rhoades, an upscale department store based in Richmond, where Ellis had often shopped for clothes and gifts when he was a teenager.

Ellis stocked the college department exclusively with preppie clothes designed by John Meyer of Norwich, Connecticut. Each year, Ellis spent nearly $1,000,000 on Meyer's designs, making Miller & Rhoades one of the company's largest accounts. Impressed by the selections Ellis made, the designer began grilling him about style trends. In 1967 Ellis became a merchandiser for John Meyer and moved to New York.

In 1974 John Meyer died of cancer, and Ellis moved to the Vera Companies, where he worked as sportswear merchandiser. Vera specialized in designing polyester double-knit pantsuits. This offended Ellis's aesthetic, and he tried to upgrade the company's image by introducing natural fabrics. In 1975 the company allowed Ellis to produce his own line under the Portfolio label. He was given only $5,000 to work with, but Ellis made the most of his opportunity. He designed 33 pieces and held a fashion show in the Vera showroom. Retailers and fashion critics were astonished by what Ellis had accomplished. The designs were eclectic, walking a fine line between being slightly conservative and slightly wild. Ellis's picture appeared on the front page of *Women's Wear Daily*, where he was touted as one of the year's up-and-coming designers.

In 1978 Perry Ellis Sportswear began production. Ellis opened his own showroom in an old bank on the corner of Seventh Avenue and 41st Street. By 1982, 75 employees were working for Perry Ellis Sportswear. But Ellis's health had begun to falter. He came down with hepatitis and was forced to lie low for six weeks. Once the hepatitis cleared up, he was struck by other maladies. Ellis kept his health problems a secret from his employees, many of whom believed that he was letting the business fall apart. "It was very hard to get excited about the line when everybody was so depressed," observed a saleswoman who worked for the company. "You'd try to be enthusiastic, but inside you were feeling like you were on the Titanic."

While battling constant health problems, Ellis was also preoccupied with fathering a child. In 1984 he had a daughter, Tyler, with Barbara Gallagher, an old friend who lived in Los Angeles. Ellis's business partner, Laughlin Barker, died in January 1986. The cause of the 37 year old's death

Holding hands with his friend Mariel Hemingway at a black-tie reception, Perry Ellis looks well dressed in his trademark preppie clothes.

Perry Ellis and Richard Haas, of Levi Strauss and Co., prepare to meet the press to announce a new collection of active sportswear, Perry Ellis America.

was listed as lung cancer. By this time Ellis's health was also rapidly deteriorating.

Five months later, a gaunt Ellis unveiled his latest line. People who attended the show believed it would be Perry's last. When the show ended, the audience rose and gave Ellis an emotional, heartfelt standing ovation. Although he was too frail to make the traditional walk down the runway, Perry appeared briefly in the doorway of his showroom. "There was a real surge of emotion," said designer Brian Bubb, "and Perry just wanted to move toward it, to grab it. We had to pull him back, because he couldn't make it. Finally, we had to tell him, 'Okay, Perry, okay. It's time to go.'" Moments after the applause died down, Ellis collapsed and was rushed to New York Hospital. Two weeks later, he slipped into a coma. A week later, on May 30, 1986, Perry Ellis died.

1934-1967

Brian Epstein decided to check out the Beatles at the Cavern after his record store received requests for a German single, "My Bonnie," which the boys had recorded in Hamburg.

It might not be fair to say that without manager Brian Epstein the Beatles would never have become the all-time top pop music group. But his astute guidance and single-mindedness were factors in their success as much as their own talent.

Brian Samuel Epstein was born on September 19, 1934, in Liverpool, England. His family was upper middle class and Jewish. Brian was close to his mother, Queenie, who encouraged him to become an artist. He wanted to pursue art or acting. He wanted any career that kept him from going into the family-owned furniture business. But he had no success in the arts, and by his late teens, Brian was working at the family business. When his father decided to add a record department to his flagship store in Liverpool, Brian jumped at the chance to manage it. Largely because of his skill at running the business, the Epstein empire eventually included nine NEMS record stores.

A savvy predictor of future pop hits, Brian was intrigued by requests for a German record made by a local group, the Beatles. He saw them perform for the first time on November 9, 1961, at the soon-to-be-legendary Cavern Club. Electrified by their raw, energetic rock 'n' roll style, he was chagrined to find out that John Lennon, Paul McCartney, George Harrison, and the Beatles' original drummer, Pete Best, were the same lads in leather jackets who spent hours listening to new releases at NEMS without ever buying a single record.

The Beatles signed a five-year management contract with Brian on January 24, 1962. Brian had no practical experience managing a pop group, but he was sure that he would succeed. He immediately began grooming the boys for success, replacing their scruffy leather jackets with ultramodern collarless suits and curtailing their liberal use of profanity onstage. In June 1962, after several months of being turned down, Brian finally secured a record contract for the Beatles with EMI Records. Their first release, "Love Me Do," hit number 17 on the British pop charts. Beatlemania was sweeping Britain, and by late 1963 the Beatles were causing near riots wherever they performed.

In the first months of 1964, Brian's campaign to duplicate the group's success in the United States shifted into high gear. He convinced their American record label, Capitol Records, to invest $20,000 to promote "I Want to Hold Your Hand." The song reached number one on the charts in January. He booked three February appearances on the influential *Ed Sullivan Show* on CBS-TV. This all but insured the Beatles' superstar status in America.

After the Beatles became world famous, Brian outwardly lived a happy life. He had several expensive cars, including a maroon Rolls Royce, and several stately homes. He ate at the finest restaurants and gambled at the best casinos. Brian was always generous to a fault. A dedicated follower of fashion, he was voted one of Britain's ten best-dressed men in 1964, the same year he published his autobiography, *A Cellarful of Noise*.

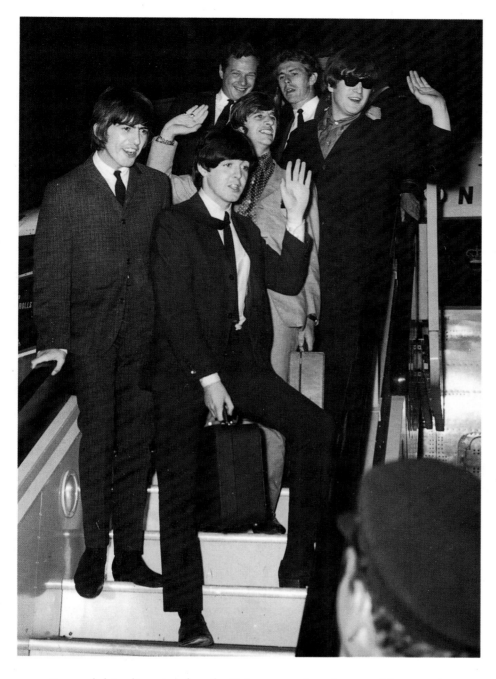

Brian was known as the fifth Beatle, and even though he and the band were from widely different backgrounds, Epstein truly enjoyed their company. It was not all business with him.

Epstein was always glad to spend time with George, but he eventually grew closer to John than any of the other Beatles.

Beneath his glittering facade, Brian was a lonely man. He was a homosexual who entered into one disastrous relationship after another. He said he was never so happy as when he and John, Paul, George, and Ringo were in the same room. But as the Beatles matured they found themselves less frequently in need of Brian's advice. Even in the best of times, he was moody and erratic, and subject to frequent, lingering bouts of depression. His mood swings were exacerbated by his liberal use of alcohol and a growing dependence on amphetamines and barbiturates.

On August 27, 1967, his Spanish butler found Brian Epstein dead in his bed at his London home. At his side was a pile of correspondence, with a number of medicine vials within arm's reach. A coroner's inquiry returned a verdict of accidental death, caused by an overdose of the drug Carbrital. In just a few weeks, Brian would have been 33 years old.

1945-1982

Rainer Werner Fassbinder was intent on making films that were politically committed and uncompromisingly antiestablishment.

Rainer Werner Fassbinder, who was born in 1945, deserves much of the credit for rebuilding German filmmaking to the level international prestige that it had attained before World War II. Ironically, his application to Berlin's prestigious film institute was rejected, but Fassbinder was determined to be a filmmaker and produced many films on shoestring budgets of only $25,000. Fassbinder often wore many different hats when he was working on a movie. For many of his early films, he served as director, writer, producer, and actor. Between 1969 and 1982, Fassbinder directed 37 movies, including *Lola*, a remake of *The Blue Angel*. This movie cost $10,000,000 to produce, and at the time it was Germany's most expensive film. In addition to directing, Fassbinder was a prolific writer. He wrote 37 screenplays, 15 plays that he also directed, and countless radio scripts.

Filmmaking was Fassbinder's passion, and his personal life floundered as a result. His parents had divorced when he was five years old, and he felt that this had left him permanently scarred and incapable of truly loving another person. Immediately following his parents' breakup, Rainer lived with his mother, but when she remarried, his new stepfather insisted Fassbinder move in with his father, a wealthy landowner and slumlord. When Fassbinder was a teenager, his father gave him the job of collecting outrageously high rents from the poverty-stricken Turkish tenants who lived in his buildings. When his mother's second marriage ended in divorce, Fassbinder returned to her home. A short while later she took a new lover; he was a domineering 17 year old who foolishly tried to play the role of stepfather to the teenage Fassbinder.

Fassbinder's romantic relationships were usually destructive. Armin Meier, with whom he shared a home in Munich for several years, was overly dependent on Fassbinder and accused him of neglect. While Fassbinder was on a trip to Paris, which he visited frequently, a despondent Meier hanged himself in their home. Rainer's mother discovered the body. Several years earlier, Hedi ben Salem, another of Fassbinder's lovers, also hanged himself, after going on a rampage in Berlin and stabbing three people. Swiss movie director Daniel Schmid, an early lover of Fassbinder, told an interviewer that "Rainer was an unhappy man who hurled himself into his work but had a low personal opinion of himself. He could not believe people could love him. All his life, Rainer thought he was ugly. The basis for his new friendship was always: You are a pig, and I am a pig."

Rainer's personal habits were extremely self-destructive. He abused alcohol and frequently used such mood-altering drugs as LSD, uppers, downers, and cocaine. Friends reported that he often smoked as many as four packs of cigarettes a day. Despite his suicidal behavior, Rainer would often tell his friends that he was afraid of dying.

On the last night of his life, June 10, 1982, Fassbinder phoned Daniel Schmid in Paris and claimed that he had flushed his entire cache of drugs down the toilet, except for one last line of cocaine. After the phone call, Fass-

On the set of *Querelle* in 1982, Fassbinder drinks a toast with Jeanne Moreau and Brad Davis.

binder spent the rest of the evening sitting in bed, making notes on his next film project. A videotape of the movie *20,000 Years in Sing Sing* played on the bedroom television.

The following morning, when friends were unable to contact Fassbinder, they called the police to investigate. Entering his home, they found Fassbinder's body in bed. He had apparently died from a heart attack. On the nearby nightstand were cocaine, pills, and whiskey.

Discussing his work in an interview with writer Boze Hadleigh, Fassbinder said, "My work is what I love, but the subjects are today, they are German, continental. Not love stories with pretty music. When I make films about hope, it is love stories I am making. Because I do not make pretty, long-to-make films, it does not mean I am not romantic. I try for romance, but usually in today's world, one fails here."

1896-1940

Before his first novel was published, F. Scott Fitzgerald was unable to place any of his short stories in magazines. The enormous popularity of *This Side of Paradise* changed this almost overnight.

F. Scott Fitzgerald was born in St. Paul, Minnesota, on September 24, 1896, and named for his famous ancestor Francis Scott Key, the author of "The Star-Spangled Banner." As a young boy, Scott was coddled by his strong-willed mother who placed all her hope for the family's future in her only son. Scott's father was a dreamer who struggled to make ends meet and was constantly criticized by his wife for his failures. Even though his family was far from wealthy, Scott attended the toniest Catholic schools in St. Paul, where he tried to compensate for his ineptitude in athletics and his working-class background by studying hard and affecting a superior air. He developed an early love of acting and wrote several plays. His poems and stories were often published in school magazines.

When Scott was ready for college, his mother's sister offered to pay for his tuition if he would attend Georgetown University in Washington, D.C. His mother wanted Scott to stay at home and go to the University of Minnesota. During the spring of 1913, Scott's grandmother died, leaving his family a large inheritance. Scott could now choose any school he wanted, and he decided on Princeton because it had the best student theater company in the country.

At Princeton Fitzgerald wrote musicals for the Triangle Club, which toured the country with as much fanfare as a Broadway show. The critics applauded Fitzgerald's lyrics, but in his daily studies, he fared poorly. He wrote to his mother that his English professors were dull and insipid. They thought he was arrogant and disinterested. By the end of his sophomore year, he was told that his grades were too low for him to continue.

After spending some time in St. Paul, Scott returned to Princeton for the fall term in 1916, but in October 1917 he joined the Army. Fitzgerald was commissioned a second lieutenant in the infantry, but he was never sent overseas. Scott first reported to Fort Leavenworth, Kansas, then to Camp Taylor, Kentucky, then Camp Gordon, Georgia, and finally to Camp Sheridan, Alabama. As an officer, he wore high boots and spurs that appealed to his sense of grandeur. They also appealed to a young woman named Zelda Sayre whom he met at a country club dance in Montgomery. Zelda and Scott fell passionately in love, and memories of their first summer together form the heart of much of Fitzgerald's writing.

After the Armistice was signed, Fitzgerald moved to New York City without his fiance. There he gathered 122 rejection slips for his stories and

In 1926 Scott, Scottie, and Zelda sailed for France, where many American writers and artists were living to escape taxes, prohibition, and provincialism.

wrote billboard slogans for the Barron Collier Advertising Agency. Scott continually pleaded with Zelda to marry him, but she hesitated because she was unsure of his reliability. Finally, after a three week bender and more rejection slips, Zelda broke off the engagement, and Fitzgerald fled to his parents' home in St. Paul to revise the novel that he had started at Princeton. In 1920 Scribners published *This Side of Paradise*, the first American novel to portray the pleasure-seeking generation of the Roaring Twenties. Scott experienced a meteoric rise in New York literary circles that also brought about the sudden acceptance of his short stories.

Fitzgerald was now able to convince Zelda to come to New York and marry him. They became the darling couple of high society and spent money lavishly. To pay the bills, Fitzgerald began to write stories for the pulp press. Although he had less time for serious writing, Scott published his second novel, *The Beautiful and the Damned*, in 1922. Scribners also brought out two collections of Fitzgerald's short stories, *Flappers and Philosophers* and *Tales of the Jazz Age*. The Fitzgeralds' daughter, Frances, whom they called Scottie, was born in 1921.

The Great Gatsby, the story of a wealthy bootlegger caught up in the moral emptiness of American society in the 1920s, was published in 1925. By that time the Fitzgeralds were deeply in debt and battling constantly with each other. Zelda flirted dangerously with Scott's friends. He felt distracted in her presence but did not trust her when she was away from him. The emotional seesaw drove him to excessive drinking. Hoping a change of scene would improve their situation, the Fitzgeralds went to Europe, where they partied with Ernest Hemingway and scores of other American expatriates.

During the nine stressful years after *Gatsby* was published, Fitzgerald watched his popularity ebb and his wife become institutionalized for manic depression, but in 1934 Fitzgerald completed *Tender Is the Night*, the second of his three major works. The book is a beautifully written account of the gradual but tragic decline of several glamorous Americans in Europe. For all its remarkable descriptive passages, *Tender Is the Night* was a commercial failure. During the Depression, American readers were too much mired in the harsh realities of survival to want to spend time reading about the excesses of the Jazz Age.

Disappointed in the novel's reception, the Fitzgeralds returned to America. Scott went to Hollywood where he earned money writing scripts. There, he fell in love with gossip columnist Sheilah Graham and lived quietly with her for the rest of his life. Zelda's mental illness worsened, and she went from one institution to another without any relief. In 1940 Fitzgerald made a last courageous effort to write a novel. He was debilitated by alcoholism and depressed by the loss of his popularity, but his work on *The Last Tycoon* is masterful. He never completed the novel about a would-be tycoon who always played harder than he worked, so Fitzgerald never regained the acclaim he had lost. On December 21, 1940, F. Scott Fitzgerald was visiting a friend in North Hollywood, when he fell over dead from a heart attack. In 1948 Zelda Fitzgerald died in a fire at Highland Hospital in Asheville, North Carolina, where she was being treated for her mental illness.

This photograph of Scott Fitzgerald was taken in 1928 while he was living in Paris and working on *Tender Is the Night*.

From the day she was born, June 10, 1922, show business was Judy Garland's life. She was named Frances Ethel Gumm by her parents, Frank and Ethel. The Gumms were a vaudeville team who operated the New Grand, the only theater in their hometown, Grand Rapids, Minnesota. Between double features they performed their act, which included Frances's two older sisters, Virginia and Mary Jane.

At the age of three, Frances, billed as Baby Gumm, made her debut singing "Jingle Bells," accompanied by Ethel, who played the piano. The audience was immediately captivated by the small child's big booming voice. Sensing their delight, Frances remained on stage, repeating chorus after chorus of "Jingle Bells." Finally, her father appeared and dragged her off the stage. The following day Frances was back, repeating "Jingle Bells," the only song she knew. Standing in the wings, Frank watched the magic that transpired between Baby Gumm and the audience and realized it would be pointless ever to drag her off the stage again.

In 1927 the Gumms moved to Lancaster, California, a small town north of Los Angeles, to run the town's only theater. Ethel and Frank frequently took their young daughters to Los Angeles, where they found work on radio programs and in stage shows. By the time she was 10 years old, Frances was appearing solo at the Coconut Grove. When the Gumms' marriage broke up in 1933, Ethel moved to Los Angeles, where she registered Frances and Virginia in a school for performing children. Mary Jane remained in Lancaster with Frank. The separation hit Frances the hardest. At night she always included a special prayer for her bickering parents.

During the summer of 1934, Ethel toured the country with her three daughters. While performing at the Oriental Theater in Chicago, Ethel met

1922-1969

In 1962 Judy Garland was the voice of Mewsette in the animated musical feature *Gay Purr-ee*. At that time Warner Bros. released this publicity photo.

Judy's performance in the 1954 movie *A Star Is Born* is a classic. She was nominated for an Oscar but lost to Grace Kelly for *The Country Girl*.

In 1937 Judy was cast opposite Mickey Rooney for the first time in *Thoroughbreds Don't Cry*. They made nine moves together before Judy starred in *The Wizard of Oz.*

Judy Garland, the little girl with the big voice, was featured on broadcasts of *Jack Oakie's College* over the WABC-Columbia network.

Opposite:
A studio portrait from the late 1930s promotes the image of Judy Garland as a wholesome girl next door.

entertainer George Jessel. Impressed by the Gumm sisters, Jessel suggested they that they change their name, and the Garland sisters were born. Frances also acquired a new first name: Judy. Soon, the Garland sisters were being represented by William Morris, a leading talent agency. A review of the trio in *Variety* in November 1934 singled out Judy's incredibly loud voice as the act's best aspect.

In August 1935 the Garland sisters performed their last show together. Judy was branching out on her own. Several weeks earlier she had auditioned for Louis B. Mayer, the president of MGM. Her performance of "Zing Went the Strings of My Heart" wowed Mayer, who quickly arranged a screen test for her. Judy was signed as a contract player, earning a starting salary of $100 a week. Judy's success was marred by tragedy when her father died suddenly.

On the MGM lot, Judy attended classes with other young performers, including Mickey Rooney, Lana Turner, Ava Gardner, and Ann Rutherford. They became her close friends and substitute family. Louis Mayer took on the role of patriarch, but his methods of handling his youngsters were unorthodox. Noticing that Judy was gaining weight, he ordered a studio doctor to prescribe diet pills, beginning Judy's lifelong battle with drug dependency.

Judy's weight problem also made Mayer reluctant to cast her in movies. By 1937 she had only three screen credits: a short, *Every Sunday,* and two features, *Pigskin Parade* and *Thoroughbreds Don't Cry*. Her career took an

In her most famous role as Dorothy in *The Wizard of Oz*, Judy wipes the tears of the Cowardly Lion, played by Bert Lahr, who is sad because he has no heart.

upward swing when she was cast as Sophie Tucker's daughter in *Broadway Melody of 1938*. Her engaging, heartfelt performance of the sentimental tune "Dear Mr. Gable" was praised lavishly in the press. Critics were not Judy's only fans. People everywhere flooded the studio with letters demanding to see more of "that teenager with the crush on Clark Gable." Judy was suddenly in demand. She appeared in a string of Andy Hardy movies, which starred Mickey Rooney, as well as several other MGM pictures. But Judy continued to struggle with her weight and began to rely heavily on diet pills.

In 1938 Judy landed a role that was originally intended for Shirley Temple. She was cast as Dorothy in *The Wizard of Oz*, MGM's big-budget musical adaptation of Frank Baum's children's novel. The movie's release the following year elevated Judy to superstar status. Newspapers reported that fans were returning to theaters dozens of times to hear Judy sing "Over the Rainbow." She became so closely associated with the role that late in her career she revealed to an audience she had performed "Over the Rainbow" 12,380 times.

The magnitude of her success following *The Wizard of Oz* overwhelmed Judy. Besides constantly struggling to maintain her weight, Judy began suffering from insomnia. Once again, the studio doctor supplied the remedy. A quick scribble on a prescription pad was all it took for uppers and downers to become part of Judy's drug regimen. She also attempted to alleviate the stress in her life with frequent visits to a psychiatrist.

In 1940 the Academy of Motion Picture Arts and Sciences presented Judy with a special Oscar for her performance in *The Wizard of Oz*. MGM acknowledged her success by raising her salary to $2,000 a week. Gossip columnists gushed about her romances with young actors Jackie Cooper and Robert Stack. They were unaware that Judy had begun an affair with Tyrone Power, who was nine years her senior. Concerned about a scandal, Mayer laid down the law and Judy had to stop seeing Power. But in 1941 19-year-old Judy eloped with David Rose, a 31-year-old musician. Mayer disapproved of the union and saw to it that Judy was kept busy with work. Besides embarking on an extensive USO tour, Judy also starred in *Meet Me in St. Louis*. A year and a half after they eloped, Judy and Rose separated. In 1945 they divorced.

One week after the divorce, Judy married film director Vincent Minnelli. A year later, she gave birth to their daughter, Liza. Now that Judy was a mother, Minnelli made her promise to stay away from pills. In 1947 she began work on *The Pirate*, directed by Minnelli. Judging by her erratic performance, it soon became clear to a disheartened Minnelli that Judy was unable to keep her promise and had slipped back into relying on pills. She often arrived late at the studio, and some days she did not show up at all. Realizing that Judy was out of control, Minnelli had her admitted to a sanatorium in Los Angeles. A short while later, she was transferred to the Riggs Foundation in Massachusetts.

In 1948 a recovered Judy returned to the MGM lot to star in *Easter Parade* with Fred Astaire. By the start of her next movie, *The Barkleys of Broadway*, Judy was back on drugs. She was prone to mood swings and regularly arrived late at the studio. Unable to tolerate Judy's habitual tardiness, Mayer had her dismissed from the film. In 1949 she was tapped to star in *Annie Get Your Gun*, but shortly after filming began, she was replaced by Betty Hutton. Before beginning work on her next project, *Summer Stock*, Judy was admitted to a Boston hospital for treatment. Following her release from the hospital, the studio decided she was overweight and ordered her to lose 15 pounds. Once again, Judy turned to diet pills, which affected her behavior, causing her again to be labeled temperamental. In 1950 she was slated to star in *Royal Wedding*, but Judy was in no condition to work, and the studio suspended her on June 17. To make matters worse, she was totally broke. Three days later, Judy attempted suicide by slashing her neck with a piece of glass. MGM released Judy from her contract, and at the same time Minnelli divorced her.

After her movie career came to a screeching halt, Judy shifted gears and moved to New York. Producer Sid Luft encouraged her to concentrate on live performances. Acting as her manager, he booked her at the Palladium in London. Judy earned rave reviews and played to sold-out houses for four weeks. Luft then booked her into the RKO-Palace Theater in New York. Judy opened on October 16, 1951. When the show closed on February 24, 1952, it had broken the Palace's attendance record. Once again, Judy was back on top. She was also falling in love with Luft. In early 1952 Judy and Sid Luft married. The following December, her second daughter, Lorna, was born. A month later, Judy's mother died. Sensational accounts of Ethel's

In 1963 CBS gave Judy her own television variety show, but the series was canceled during its first season when it failed to gain a large enough audience.

death speculated that Judy had abandoned her mother, leaving her to spend her last years toiling in a factory.

In 1953 Luft negotiated Judy's return to Hollywood. Warner Bros. signed her to star in its remake of *A Star Is Born*. Judy's powerful performance in the movie netted her an Academy Award nomination for best actress. Judy did not win the Oscar, but that spring she gave birth to her son, Joey. Despite her success with *A Star Is Born*, Judy received no offers for other movie roles. Instead, Luft arranged for her to star in her first television special, which aired in 1955.

Judy was again struggling with her weight and resumed taking pills. Audiences at her shows were not pleased with the results. Rather than giving top-notch performances, Judy's voice faltered and she forgot lyrics and appeared spacey onstage. Finally, in the late 1950s, Judy booked herself into a New York hospital for treatment. "I went to pieces," Judy candidly revealed to an interviewer. "All I wanted to do was eat and hide. I lost all my self-confidence for 10 years. I suffered agonies of stage fright. People had to literally push me onto the stage."

In early 1961 Judy felt that she had recovered enough to return to the stage. The Palladium Theater in London was her first stop. On April 23, 1961, she kicked off a 16-city tour of the United States with a one-night performance at New York's Carnegie Hall. The audiences responded to Judy's splendid performance with a rousing, emotional standing ovation. That same year director Stanley Kramer cast Judy in a supporting role as a Jewish housewife in *Judgment at Nuremberg*. Despite a second Oscar nomination, the Hollywood studios continued to ignore Judy, and she went back on the road, performing live.

By 1963 the stress of constant touring was beginning to affect Judy's performances. When CBS offered her her own weekly television series, she jumped at the opportunity. For the first time in years, she would be able to spend her evenings at home with her children. Judy taped 26 episodes of her series, before receiving yet another blow. CBS dropped the show because she had not garnered a large enough audience in a time slot that pitted her against NBC's top-rated *Bonanza*.

Judy's marriage to Luft ended in 1965. A concert she performed in Australia was so disastrous the audience reportedly booed her off the stage. She was married briefly to Mark Herron, a struggling actor, who was 14 years her junior. In 1967 Judy was cast in the movie version of Jacqueline Susann's novel *Valley of the Dolls*, but shortly before filming began, she was abruptly replaced by Susan Hayward. In 1968 she was evicted from the St. Moritz because she was unable to pay her $1,800 hotel bill.

In 1969 Judy married for the fifth time. Referring to her new husband, Mickey Deans, a 35-year-old restaurant manager, Judy said, "Finally, finally, I am loved." Although her health had deteriorated, a gallant Judy made a brief concert tour of Scandinavia. On June 22, 1969, Mickey Deans discovered his wife dead in the bathroom of their cottage on Cadogan Lane in London. An autopsy determined that her death was accidental, the result of a barbiturate overdose.

Judy was photographed with her 20-year-old daughter Liza in London in 1966.

Marvin Gaye was Motown's duet king, performing joyous love songs with the label's best female vocalists. He was sensuous and shocking, and he was always socially relevant. No one could ever predict what he would sing about next. Marvin was always unpredictable.

He was born on April 2, 1939, in Washington, D.C. Even as a young boy, he wasn't afraid to stand out from the crowd. He enjoyed singing solos with the choir at the Pentecostal church where his father was the minister. In high school he studied drums and piano. When he heard that singer Harvey Fuqua was going to judge the high-school talent contest, Marvin figured he would get the judge's attention by singing "The Ten Commandments of Love," a song Fuqua had made popular. Marvin's audacity paid off; he did not win the contest, but his group impressed Fuqua anyway.

To please his father, Marvin joined the United States Air Force. He would have preferred to get on with his music career after high school. Marvin stayed in the Air Force less than a year; he was discharged for psychological reasons. This was the first acknowledgement of his problem with the mood swings that was to plague him throughout his life.

As soon as he got back to Washington, Marvin joined a vocal group called the Marquees. When Fuqua's group, the Moonglows, needed new singers, he hired the Marquees. Marvin can be heard on the Moonglows' 1959 release "Mama Loocie." In 1960 Fuqua disbanded the group and went to Detroit, where Berry Gordy signed him for his new label, Motown. Marvin followed Fuqua to Motown. Fuqua married Gordy's sister Dawn and produced many Motown hits. Marvin married Gordy's other sister, Anna.

Gaye was content as a session drummer at Motown, but after hearing Marvin's voice bring life to a party, Gordy signed his brother-in-law to a recording contract. After three misses Marvin scored in 1962 with "Stubborn Kind of Fellow," which is backed by Martha and the Vandellas. After a string of successes, it was clear that Marvin could effectively add his signature to any style, but Motown's marketing strategy typecast the label's artists. Marvin was told to team up with Mary Wells and warble love songs. After a pair of modest hits, Wells quit the label, and Marvin was paired briefly with Kim Weston.

The third time around, Gaye got the perfect partner, Tammi Terrell. They toured together and recorded one hit after another. In 1967 Tammi was onstage singing with Marvin when she suddenly collapsed in his arms. Three years later, she was dead from a brain tumor. Marvin's next release was the poignant "The End of Our Road."

Marvin stopped performing for a year and made no public appearances. With virtually no fanfare, he resurfaced to present a vastly different kind of music. Motown executives thought his new stuff would never sell, but Marvin used his still-considerable influence to get the label to record the introspective and socially relevant "What's Going On," "Mercy Mercy Me (The Ecology)," and "Inner City Blues (Make We Wanna Holler)." He also

1939-1984

During the 1970s Marvin Gaye shifted the focus of his music first to impassioned protest songs about Vietnam and the environment and then to purely erotic songs.

Marvin Gaye was first and foremost a tenor with a three-octave range. During the 1960s he preferred romantic ballads, but he also recorded upbeat tunes and dance hits.

took a new partner, his old and trusted friend Diana Ross. But musically, Marvin's heart was elsewhere. He hit number one in 1973 with "Let's Get It On," a song that many radio stations refused to play because of its suggestive lyrics.

Gaye's marriage fell apart in the mid 1970s. He was frequently moody and often disappeared to Europe for months at a time, ignoring any commitments that would have kept him at home. Marvin went bankrupt, but the judge who was handling his divorce instructed him to record an album to raise the $600,000 he owed in alimony. With his personal life in shreds, Marvin left Motown and began recording for Columbia.

With the release of *Midnight Love* in 1982, Marvin was back on tour, playing to packed houses. On April 1, 1984, he visited his 70-year-old father at his home in Los Angeles. Marvin's life ended abruptly with two shots from his father's gun. There had been an argument and a fistfight, and suddenly the unpredictable Marvin Gaye was dead.

▪ LOU GEHRIG ▪

Fifty years after his death, Lou Gehrig, baseball's "Iron Horse," still holds a major league record for the 2,130 consecutive games that he played for the New York Yankees between 1925 and 1939. He also has a .340 career batting average, making him one of the greatest hitters of all time. Sadly, Lou's life story is tragic. He was a clean-living, enormously successful athlete, who was admired by both his teammates and the opposing players, but he was cut down in the prime of life.

Henry Louis Gehrig was born in the Yorkville section of Manhattan on June 19, 1903. His parents, Heinrich and Christina, were German immigrants. Of their four children, Lou was the only one who survived to adulthood. Growing up, Lou was something of a mama's boy. He lived with his parents until he married, when he was 30 years old. Lou attended New York public schools, where he excelled as an athlete. When he was only 11, Lou swam across the Hudson River. He went to the city's High School of Commerce, where he starred in baseball, football, and swimming.

In his senior year, Lou's school won New York's public school baseball championship. They played Chicago's best high school team, Lane Tech, in Chicago's Wrigley Field in 1920. The game was a portent of what was to come: With the bases loaded and two outs in the ninth inning, Lou crushed a 3-2 pitch over the right field wall to win the game.

To fulfill his parents' dream, Lou enrolled at New York's Columbia University in 1922. Because he had briefly played for a professional baseball club the preceding summer, Lou was barred from athletic competition at Columbia for a year. After sitting the year out, Lou starred on the college's baseball and football squads, earning the nickname Columbia Lou.

When his father lost his job and his mother fell ill, Lou decided to leave college for a professional baseball career. In June 1923 the New York Yankees signed him to a minor league contract. He was assigned to the team's Hartford, Connecticut, farm club, where he played for two seasons as a power-hitting first baseman. That was just what the parent team was looking for, and Lou was inserted into the starting Yankee lineup on June 1, 1925, substituting for their regular first baseman, Wally Pipp. For the next 14 years, Lou did not miss a single game.

Even though Lou made an immediate impression in the majors, leading the American League with 20 triples in his second season, it was in 1927 that the six-foot, 210-pound left-hander blossomed as a slugger. Hitting cleanup in Murderer's Row, as the Yankee lineup was called, he challenged teammate Babe Ruth for the league's home-run title. By the end of the season, Lou had hit 47 homers to the Babe's 60. That year Lou hit .373 and set a major league record by racking up 175 RBIs. Not surprisingly, Lou was voted the league's Most Valuable Player. He also helped the 1927 Yankees—arguably the best team ever to play the game—to sweep the Pittsburgh Pirates in the World Series. True to form, Lou had almost decided to sit out the entire series to stay at his ill mother's side.

1903-1941

This photograph was taken in June 1925 when Columbia Lou first reported to the New York Yankees. The team's manager, Miller Huggins, told an interviewer that he was delighted with his new prospect.

For 13 consecutive seasons, Lou knocked home more than 100 runs, and he slugged 46 home runs with 184 RBIs in 1931. On June 3, 1932, Lou hit four home runs in one game against the Philadelphia Athletics, setting another major league record.

Lou was a quiet man, who was less flamboyant than his teammate Ruth. Lou was always modest about his talents. This quality made him a hero to millions of impressionable kids. In 1933 he married Eleanor Twitchell. She helped him withstand the rigors of professional baseball. On the eve of consecutive game 2,000 in 1938, Eleanor suggested that Lou was getting compulsive about the streak and advised him to end it at 1,999 games. Despite his wife's good intentions, Lou would not be deterred.

During spring training in 1939, Lou began to experience weakness and problems with coordination. To sportswriters following the Yankees, it seemed that Lou couldn't hit the ball and couldn't play defense anymore. On May 2 his consecutive game streak finally ended when he removed himself from the lineup. "It's tough to see your mates on base, have a chance to win a ball game, and not be able to do anything about it," he said.

While newspaper reporters were speculating that the streak had worn Lou out, he knew something else was causing his problems. He entered the Mayo Clinic in Rochester, Minnesota, for tests. On his 36th birthday, he was diagnosed as suffering from a rare muscular disorder, amyotrophic lateral sclerosis. The disease causes the motor neurons to degenerate, resulting in atrophying muscles, which in turn cause paralysis and ultimately death. Eleanor asked the doctors to withhold that fact about his disease from her husband.

Lou stayed with the team as the nonplaying captain for the rest of the 1939 season, receiving standing ovations from the crowd every time he took the team's lineup card to home plate before a game. On July 4, 62,000 fans crowded Yankee Stadium to honor him on Lou Gehrig Day. In his well-remembered speech to the crowd, Lou said that he considered himself "the luckiest man on the face of the earth." On his retirement from baseball at the end of the season, Lou was voted into baseball's Hall of Fame.

New York mayor Fiorello LaGuardia named Lou the city's parole commissioner. He held the job until his declining health confined him to bed. Before the Iron Horse died at home on June 2, 1941, at the age of 37, he had become so weak that he was unable to swallow a mouthful of water. His universal renown was so great that after his death amyotrophic lateral sclerosis became known as Lou Gehrig's Disease.

Lou Gehrig slugged a total of 23 grand-slam home runs, topped the .300 batting mark for 12 straight seasons, and established an American League record of 184 RBIs in 1931.

Lou Gehrig was so popular with fans that in 1934, when Goudey Gum Company released its second set of baseball cards, the Iron Horse was pictured on every one of them.

1945-1979

As a child, Lowell George played harmonica. In high school he switched to flute, then oboe and baritone saxophone. Finally, he found rhythm guitar and stuck with that instrument throughout his career.

His friend Jackson Browne once dubbed Lowell George the Orson Welles of rock, and he was not just talking about Lowell's considerable girth. As the founder and leader of the rock group Little Feat, Lowell's bizarre sense of humor, matched with his peerless musicianship, made the group one of the most critically acclaimed acts of the 1970s. Orson Welles was considered a genius by almost everyone who ever worked with him, so was Lowell George.

The son of a wealthy Los Angeles furrier, Lowell was born April 13, 1945, into a world of glamor. Movie star Errol Flynn was the family's next-door neighbor in Laurel Canyon. W.C. Fields dropped by the house on frequent visits. Lowell's privileged childhood helped to produce the absurd sense of humor that was one of his most endearing traits.

Lowell's first musical instrument was a harmonica, and he appeared with his brother on Ted Mack's *Original Amateur Hour* in a harmonica duet. At Hollywood High School, George played the flute. He developed an early interest in jazz, and because he was underage, he had to sneak into clubs to hear his jazz idols, especially saxophonists Sonny Rollins and Roland Kirk. He also could play oboe and baritone saxophone, and once joined in on a Frank Sinatra recording session. Lowell started college at Valley Junior College, but he dropped out to form a rock band after attending a Byrds' concert and hearing the group play "Mr. Tambourine Man." Years later, the Byrds recorded one of Lowell's songs, "Truck Stop Girl."

George switched from wind instruments to guitar, attributing the change to the influence of blues musicians Howlin' Wolf and Muddy Waters. After he started playing guitar, Lowell went through a series of Los Angeles bands before hooking up with Frank Zappa and the Mothers of Invention. His brief stint with the group ended when Zappa suggested Lowell would be better off leading his own group. He even suggested a name for the band—Little Feat.

As Little Feat's main singer, songwriter, and guitarist, Lowell fused his funky rhythm-and-blues rock style with memorable lyric images. The critics adored the group, and they also built a strong following of loyal fans. Singing with Little Feat, Lowell developed into one of rock's finest vocalists, while his slide guitar style was so unique that many people recognize it after hearing just one or two notes.

The group's albums *Sailin' Shoes, Dixie Chicken,* and *Feats Don't Fail Me Now* sold well, but Little Feat made a go of it only by nonstop touring. Constantly being on the road produced a lot of friction between Lowell and some of the other members of the group who resented his authority. His solution was to step out of the limelight on the next few Little Feat albums. During this time he produced albums for such artists as Bonnie Raitt and the Grateful Dead. Lowell also began work on a solo album that was to occupy him on and off for the next few years, while he remained with Little Feat.

In 1978 Little Feat's double live album, *Waiting for Columbus*, finally made them major rock radio stars. Unfortunately, the group's internal dissension came to a head, and they broke up not long after the album's release. Lowell's solo album, *Thanks I'll Eat It Here*, came out in March 1979. It is an esoteric collection that showcases his singing more than his guitar playing or songwriting, much to the disappointment of some of his fans. Lowell put together a new band and toured later that year to help promote the album.

The night after playing a concert in Washington, D.C., Lowell experienced chest pains. His wife, Elizabeth, summoned paramedics. Lowell George was dead on arrival at the hospital on June 29, 1979, the victim of heart failure. He left behind his wife, four children, and an enduring body of work that attests to his greatness. Nine years after Lowell's death, the remaining members of Little Feat re-formed the group with a new lead vocalist who sounds uncannily like Lowell.

Lowell George shaped the music of Little Feat with his bluesy voice, slide guitar, and playful lyrics.

1942-1970

Jimi Hendrix picked up a lot of
tricks from T. Bone Walker,
Johnny Guitar Watson, and
other black musicians who
turned him on to playing guitar
behind his back, with his teeth,
and in any other outrageous
way he could dream up.

When he was born on November 27, 1942, in Seattle, Washington, Jimi's mother named him John Allen Hendrix. His father was away at war; his mother was too ill and alcoholic to care for her baby, so he was sent to live with relatives in Berkeley, California. When his dad returned home, he renamed him James Marshall Hendrix, divorced his wife, and took on the task of raising his son alone.

One day Al Hendrix noticed his 13-year-old son holding a broom and strumming its imaginary strings. He found an old ukulele for him to play and eventually replaced it with a five-dollar Silvertone acoustic guitar. Jimi was left handed and found the new guitar hard to play until he reversed the strings. Al couldn't afford guitar lessons, but he never discouraged his son from pursuing something he obviously loved. Even when Hendrix could afford left-handed guitars, he always used a modified right-handed instrument.

In 1959 Jimi dropped out of high school and enlisted in the Army, but he soon became disenchanted with military service. His unit, the 101st Airborne Division, was stationed in Ft. Campbell, Kentucky, and Hendrix spent all his free time hanging out in nearby Nashville, where he discovered the blues. After hurting his back on a training jump, Hendrix was honorably discharged from the Army. He immediately got work as a side man on the rhythm-and-blues circuit, honing his craft but making little or no money. Jimi's first big break came in 1963, during a stay in Vancouver. He met Richard Penniman, better known as Little Richard, who taught the inexperienced musician the value of showmanship.

Hendrix eventually grew tired of fronting for the singer and moved on to New York City, hoping to get a break. Through his friend Curtis Knight, Hendrix discovered Greenwich Village and its hip music scene. The Who, Bob Dylan, and the Yardbirds left indelible impressions on Jimi. At this time he began experimenting with LSD and marijuana.

In 1966, while he was fronting his own band, Jimmy James & the Blue Flames, at the Cafe Wha?, John Hammond Jr. approached Hendrix about the Flames playing backup for him at the Cafe Au Go Go. Hendrix agreed and during the show's finale, Hammond let Jimi cut loose on Bo Diddley's "I'm a Man." Jimi played with his teeth, behind his back, on his head, and in any other position he could think of. The sounds emanating from his Stratocaster were none anyone had ever heard before. The crowd went wild. A star was born.

The raw power of Jimi Hendrix
on his Fender Stratocaster
redefined the way in which rock
guitar should be played.

Linda Keith, the girlfriend of the Stones' lead axe man, Keith Richards, was one of Hendrix's biggest fans. She told her friend Chas Chandler, an aspiring band manager, about Hendrix. When he heard Jimi play, Chandler asked Hendrix to come with him to London. In England, not America, Hendrix found his home. After auditioning members for his band, Hendrix and Chandler decided on Noel Redding, bass, and John "Mitch" Mitchell, drums. Chandler made a quick change in Hendrix's first name. Enter the Jimi Hendrix Experience.

Hendrix took England by storm, and by the summer of 1967, he was ready to return to the United States. At the Monterey International Pop Festival, a mixup backstage forced Hendrix to follow the Who onstage. The mayhem that ensued is a rock legend. After a superb set by the Who, Hendrix took over and tore up the house. He used every nuance, trick, and ploy he knew. Townshend smashed his guitar; Hendrix burned his. Rock music had a new prince of chaos.

Hendrix's career skyrocketed. The Experience's first two albums, *Are You Experienced?* and *Axis: Bold As Love,* catapulted him to the top of the charts and made him the highest-paid rocker in the business. Hendrix was doing more and more acid and slowly losing touch with the friends that had helped him the most. In February 1968 Chas Chandler quit in disgust, selling out to his partner Mike Jeffrey for $300,000. In September 1968 the Experience released their most successful album to date, *Electric Ladyland.*

On August 18, 1969, Woodstock happened. The Jimi Hendrix Experience was to be the closing night's headliner. Because of the immense crowd and logistical problems, Hendrix ended up playing on the morning of the fourth day. Only 30,000 people had stayed on in the mud and rain, but they were treated to musical history. Hendrix's searing rendition of "The Star-Spangled Banner" became the anthem of the counterculture. Hendrix's music perfectly captured the volatility of the times.

After Woodstock the Experience broke up, and a new lineup featuring Hendrix's old friends Billy Cox, bass, and Buddy Miles, drums, recorded his last album, *Band of Gypsys,* released in May 1970. Jimi was preparing to collaborate with Chas Chandler and jazz arranger Gil Evans on a release tentatively titled *First Rays of the New Rising Sun.* On the night of September 17, 1970, in London Hendrix took some sleeping pills that had been prescribed for his girlfriend Monika Danneman. Sometime during the night, Hendrix threw up, but Danneman, thinking he was all right, left to get cigarettes. When she returned, she could not wake Hendrix. Monika called an ambulance and then watched helplessly as they took Jimi Hendrix away. He never regained consciousness.

Jimi's life was brief, but his impact on rock guitar is still being felt. Hendrix was a true success story, earning every bit of fame that came to him. He struggled against impossible odds and won. His tunes, particularly "Purple Haze," "Foxy Lady," and "Fire," not only helped define a generation, but they set the course for a new era of rock music. Vernon Reid, lead guitar for Living Colour, said it best: "Jimi helped define the colorlessness of the artist and the colorfulness of the music."

Jimi Hendrix spent the early 1960s playing backup for B.B. King, Ike and Tina Turner, Solomon Burke, Jackie Wilson, Tommy Tucker, Sam Cooke, Little Richard, Wilson Pickett, the Isley Brothers, and King Curtis.

Jim Henson, a tall, soft-spoken man, gave the world the precious gift of love and laughter with his Muppets. Miss Piggy, Big Bird, Bert and Ernie, Oscar the Grouch, and Kermit the Frog are the dear friends of children and grownups around the world. Through his pioneering work on public television's *Sesame Street*, Jim's characters have helped teach millions of preschoolers their ABCs, and *The Muppet Show* proved that Kermit and his friends were just as appealing to adults.

Jim was born on September 24, 1936, in Greenville, Mississippi. His dad was an agronomist who worked for the United States Department of Agriculture. When Jim's father was transferred to the bureau's Washington, D.C., headquarters, the Henson family moved to Hyattsville, Maryland, where Jim discovered puppetry. Between high school and college at the University of Maryland, Henson got a job as a puppeteer at NBC's Washington affiliate, WRC-TV. His five-minute show was called *Sam and His Friends*, and when the program won an Emmy in 1958 for the best local entertainment show, Jim began seriously to consider making a career out of his Muppets. "All the time I was in school, I didn't take it seriously," he later admitted. "I mean, it didn't seem to be the sort of thing a grown man works at for a living."

In 1959 Jim married his college sweetheart, Jane Nebel. She became his first puppetry partner and continued to assist him for many years. The couple had five children, Lisa, Cheryl, Brian, John Paul, and Heather, and some of the kids have also worked for Jim, although each of them eventually chose separate careers.

After graduating from college, Jim began making television commercials. For many years this lucrative enterprise financed his experiments in reinventing puppetry. One character he created for a commercial, Rowlf the Dog, launched Jim's career on network television. The philosophizing Rowlf, with Jim working him and providing his voice, became a popular guest on such programs as *The Ed Sullivan Show* and *The Tonight Show*. From 1963 to 1966, Rowlf was a regular character on *The Jimmy Dean Show*.

Bernie Brillstein, Jim's agent for 30 years, recalled their first meeting. "I didn't want to see him, but up came this young Abe Lincoln wearing some kind of hippie arts-and-crafts clothes." As Brillstein was about to dismiss Henson as a nobody, his boss called and asked the agent if he had ever heard of Jim Henson and the Muppets because someone wanted to book him into Radio City Music Hall. Brillstein quickly changed his opinion of Jim Henson.

Year by year Jim's stock in the show biz world soared. In 1965 he wrote, produced, directed, and starred in *Timepiece*, an experimental film short with no Muppets that was nominated for an Academy Award. In 1968 he produced "Muppets on Puppets" for National Education Television, which named the program the year's outstanding children's show. When the ground-breaking children's program *Sesame Street* premiered on 160 educational television stations the following year, Jim and his Muppets were a

1936-1990

Jim Henson, the creator of the Muppets, and his alter ego, Kermit the Frog, cuddle three of the Muppet Babies, who have their own animated television series.

major factor in the program's success. Soon-to-be famous Henson creations including Kermit the Frog, Bert and Ernie, and Oscar the Grouch introduced film and live-action segments and taught kids their numbers and letters in creative and entertaining ways. "Kids love to learn," Henson said. "And the learning should be exciting and fun. That's what we're out to do." *Sesame Street* and the Muppets were a huge success. By the early 1970s, almost half of America's 12 million preschoolers were *Sesame Street* viewers.

Columbia Records released a series of Muppet albums, as well as the novelty single, "Rubber Duckie," which featured Jim in the guise of Ernie. In the 1970s the Muppets seemed to be everywhere. Jim and his growing support staff did a "Muppet Valentine Special" for ABC-TV, as well as "Out to Lunch" for the Children's Television Workshop, in which Kermit and his pals take over a television station.

Despite his growing fame, Jim remained as self-effacing as ever. He was self-conscious about his appearance and wore a beard to hide the scars of adolescent acne. According to his coworkers, he was an easy boss to work for. Carroll Spinney, who played Big Bird and Oscar the Grouch for 20 years, said, "Jim would never say he didn't like something. He would just go, 'Hmmm.' That was famous. And if he liked something, he would just say, 'Lovely.'" Along with critical acclaim came enormous personal wealth, which paid for the Henson family's large homes in Connecticut, Malibu, Orlando, and London. Jim also had a penchant for exotic cars and enjoyed such diversions as hot-air ballooning in France or camel riding in Egypt.

In the fall of 1976, *The Muppet Show* made its television debut. With a regular audience of 235 million, it became the most successful syndicated television series in history. Duncan Kenworthy, the head of the London production facility where the show was filmed, remembers that "Jim was as famous in the rest of the world as he was in America. In Japan he's as well known as Steven Spielberg."

The Muppet Show featured Henson's characters interacting with real-life stars. The indefatigable Miss Piggy danced "Swan Lake" with ballet star Rudolf Nureyev and sang opera with diva Beverly Sills. Jim's genius was in making his characters transcend the limitations of puppetry. Everyone loved the temperamental Miss Piggy and the woebegone Fozzie Bear. While warding off the advances of Miss Piggy and soothing the egos of dozens of other Muppet characters, Kermit the Frog was the most human of all. In 1979 Kermit starred in *The Muppet Movie*, Henson's first full-length feature film.

Henson Associates, Jim's company, had its headquarters in Manhattan. The executive suite was just down the hall from a two-story workshop where a half dozen assistants created Muppets out of 15 basic body shapes, swapping eyes, noses, and mouths to create new characters.

Miss Piggy and Kermit the Frog rehearse a scene for *The Muppet Show*, which was filmed in England and shown on televisions all over the world.

Behind the scenes at the workshop where Muppets are created, Jim Henson and his assistants give life to a new creature.

Jim poses happily with members of the cast of *Fraggle Rock*, a syndicated cable television show.

In 1981 Jim pulled the plug on *The Muppet Show*. "I wanted to quit while I was ahead," he said. "I didn't want to get stale." He returned to the big screen in 1984 with *The Muppets Take Manhattan*, in which Kermit and Miss Piggy were finally wed. In 1986 the Muppets celebrated their thirtieth anniversary, but Jim thought he had lost his golden touch when his fantasy film *Labyrinth* was a box office flop. Jane Henson said that the failure of *Labyrinth* was a great blow for Jim. He couldn't understand what he had done wrong. That same year the Hensons were legally separated, although they had lived apart for the past two years.

In 1989 Jim began negotiations to sell Henson Associates and his creative services to the Walt Disney Company for an estimated $150,000,000. His intention was to provide greater longevity for his Muppet characters. The sale also would free him to concentrate on other projects. In the spring of 1990, Jim was putting the finishing touches on plans for the June premiere of the Muppets at Disney World in Orlando, Florida. In early May he developed a respiratory infection that went untreated until it forced him into the New York Hospital emergency room on May 15. He died the next day following a severe attack of pneumonia. His doctors said that if Jim had sought medical treatment just six hours earlier, he probably would have survived.

He once said, "My hope is to leave the world a little bit better than when I got here." Millions of children and adults agree that Jim Henson did just that.

Jazz singer Billie Holiday, the beloved Lady Day, amazed her fans during her 25-year recording career with her ability to squeeze every bit of emotion out of a song's lyrics with a voice that was anything but conventional. During the late 1950s, Frank Sinatra said, "Lady Day is unquestionably the single most important influence on popular singing in the last 20 years." Unfortunately, the joy her music brought to others was largely missing from her own life.

She was born Eleanora Fagan in Baltimore, Maryland, on April 7, 1915. Her mother, Sadie Fagan, was 13 years old and unmarried. Billie never knew her father, but when Sadie married Clarence Holiday a few years later, Billie was given her stepfather's last name. Clarence was a professional musician, who soon abandoned his new family, but not before giving the future jazz singer the nickname Bill for her tomboy ways. Later, Bill became Billie.

Billie did not have much of a childhood. When she was 10 years old, she was raped by a man who lived in her mother's boardinghouse. She was consequently sent to a Catholic reform school because a judge felt that she looked "too provocative" for her age. Later, Billie followed her mother to New York, where she worked briefly as a prostitute. She was arrested for solicitation when she was only 14 years old and never returned to prostitution.

To earn her way, Billie began working as a dancer in Harlem. When her employer at the Log Cabin Club asked her if she could sing, which she had been doing all her short life, a new world opened for 15-year-old Billie Holiday. Singing for $2 a night, she quickly began to attract the attention of the city's black musicians, who were impressed by her already unique sound.

Her voice was a thin soprano in which nuance and subtlety took precedence over lung power. Her early idols were Louis Armstrong and blues singer Bessie Smith. "I always wanted Bessie's big sound and Armstrong's feeling," she once said. "But I found it didn't work with me, because I didn't have a big voice. Between the two of them I got Billie Holiday."

John Hammond, a talent scout for Columbia Records, discovered Billie at a New York club called Monette's in 1933. He later introduced her to another one of his discoveries, the up-and-coming bandleader Benny Goodman. He led the pick-up band that backed Billie on her first two record sides for Columbia, "Riffin' the Scotch" and "Your Mother's Son-In-Law."

The record sold only modestly, and Billie received a grand total of $35 for her effort. But having a record release enabled Billie to begin working in classier nightclubs. In 1935 Hammond paired Billie with pianist and bandleader Teddy Wilson. During the next five years, she recorded nearly 200 songs with Wilson's group, cementing her growing reputation as one of America's top young jazz singers.

Thanks to her friendship with saxophonist Lester Young, Billie was hired to replace Helen Humes as the featured vocalist in Count Basie's band in 1937. During her brief stint on the road with Basie, she encountered intense racism wherever she went. Things were even worse when Billie

1915-1959

Billie Holiday was given the name Lady Day by Count Basie's side man Lester Young.

jumped ship to work for Artie Shaw, becoming the first black vocalist to sing with an all-white big band. She quit the band after a New York club owner refused to let her sit on the bandstand and forced her to use a freight elevator to reach her dressing room. In 1939 Billie made her first public statement about racism with the song "Strange Fruit," a thinly veiled reference to the still-common lynchings of black men, especially in the South.

Her first husband, Jimmy Monroe, introduced Billie to heroin. "It wasn't long before I was one of the highest paid slaves around," she later wrote in her autobiography. "I was making a thousand a week, but I had about as much freedom as a field hand in Virginia a hundred years before." Billie's heroin habit dogged her for the rest of her life.

In the early 1940s, resplendent in her trademark satin gowns, Billie took center stage on her own at such upscale New York clubs as the Cotton Club. After a felony conviction for drug possession in 1944, Billie was refused a cabaret license and could not work at New York nightclubs that served alcohol. She began giving concerts instead. In 1944 Billie signed with Decca Records and recorded "Lover Man," which became one of her biggest hits. For Decca she also recorded the enduring classics "God Bless the Child" and "Them There Eyes."

Despite her success, Billie could not overcome her drug habit. She was busted again in 1947 on a narcotics charge and sentenced to one year at a prison in West Virginia. When she sang at Carnegie Hall after her release, she was convinced that more people came to see the needle scars on her arms than to hear her sing.

Billie switched to Verve Records in the early 1950s. Although she continued to record, her drug and alcohol use was beginning to take its toll on her voice. In 1957, when Billie appeared with her old friend Lester Young on a CBS-TV special, she looked much older than her age. By the end of the decade, she was living alone in New York, with a chihuahua that she fed from a baby bottle as her sole companion. Her health began to fail from years of abuse, and she was hospitalized in 1959. Even in the hospital Billie could not get any peace: She was arrested in her bed at New York's Metropolitan Hospital for possession of heroin. Billie Holiday acquired a kidney infection while she was still in the hospital and died there on July 17, 1959.

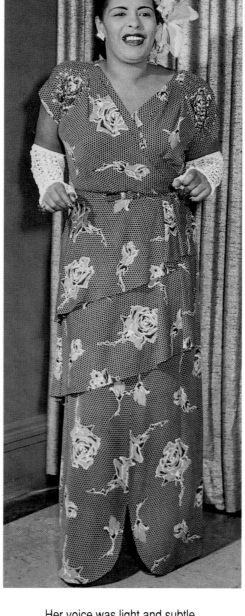

Her voice was light and subtle, and when Lady Day sang, she almost always sang with a blues feeling even though she rarely sang the blues.

During the height of her popularity in the top New York nightclubs, Billie wrote "God Bless the Child," a moving song about poverty's devastating effect on children.

After a narcotics conviction resulted in the loss of her cabaret license, Billie could no longer sing in nightclubs so she sang in concert halls, some less glamorous than others.

1921-1965

In 1950, when this photograph was taken, Judy Holliday starred in the Columbia production *Born Yesterday*, recreating her Broadway role.

Hollywood legend maintains that Judy Holliday's scene-stealing role in *Adam's Rib* was purposefully enhanced and expanded by director George Cukor, scriptwriter Garson Kanin, and star Katharine Hepburn. Their goal was to ensure that Holliday would win the starring role of Billie Dawn in the film version of *Born Yesterday*. Judy had received rave reviews for her kooky Billie Dawn in the smash Broadway comedy three years earlier, but studio head Harry Cohn was not convinced she could successfully bring the role to the screen.

Holliday's big scene in *Adam's Rib* is an interview with her attorney, Katharine Hepburn. Judy's character has shot her husband because of his infidelities. The long scene emphasizes Holliday's mastery of comic timing. Hepburn underplayed her part, giving Holliday the edge with her quirky voice and fussy gestures. The blonde newcomer stole the scene from the acclaimed star, and Cohn was persuaded to cast her as Billie Dawn, a role coveted by many actresses. Also in *Adam's Rib*, Holliday first exhibited the characteristics that would define her screen image. As the sympathetic wife of a two-timing husband, she is honest, naive, and deceptively simple-minded but never really dumb.

Born Judith Tuvim in 1921, Holliday began her show-business career when she signed on as a switchboard operator for Orson Welles's Mercury Theatre while she was still a teenager. In 1939 she formed a comedy-sketch group called the Revuers with writers Betty Comden, Adolph Green, and John Frank. Appearances in nightclubs and stints on the radio with the Revuers led to a short-lived association with 20th Century-Fox in 1944. Holliday appeared in minor roles in three forgettable movies before returning to New York to replace an ailing Jean Arthur in the stage version of *Born Yesterday*.

Billie Dawn, as she is played by Holliday, is more than the dumb blonde girlfriend of a power-hungry gangster. She is a dynamic character capable of growth and change. Cohn never regretted giving the movie role of Billie Dawn to Judy, who won an Academy Award for her performance. The movie *Born Yesterday* made Holliday a star, and the actress and the character became inextricably intertwined. The press and the movie industry oversimplified Judy's image, labeling her a dumb blonde. If Holliday seemed to play one bubbly, kooky blonde after another, at least she meticulously built each of her characters through gesture, facial expression, and vocal inflection.

In 1952, just as her movie career was taking off, Holliday was brought before the Senate Internal Security Subcommittee. She had been active in liberal organizations that later were called "communist." Postwar red-baiting hit the Hollywood film industry hard. People found to have "communist sympathies" were unofficially blacklisted by the studios. Cohn, unwilling to have his newest star ruined, hired lawyers and consultants to help clear Judy's name. It is likely that when Holliday was questioned, she adopted a persona not unlike Billie Dawn, thwarting the committee's attempts to pin

On March 29, 1951, Judy received news that she had won an Oscar for *Born Yesterday*. She met the press in a New York nightclub, wiping tears of happiness from her eyes.

Judy Holliday and Dean Martin attempt a little soft-shoe routine down by the East River in this scene from the movie *Bells Are Ringing*, which is set in Manhattan.

her down by humorously twisting the meaning of their questions. Eventually, she was cleared.

Holliday returned to Broadway in 1956 in *Bells Are Ringing*, written by her friends and former associates Comden and Green, and choreographed by Bob Fosse. Written especially for her, the story involves an operator for an answering service who gets too involved with the personal lives of her clients. Although Holliday was not a dancer, Fosse was able to use her flair for physical comedy as a basis for her dance numbers. The film version of *Bells Are Ringing*, directed by Vincent Minnelli, kept the essence of Holliday's character but unfortunately left out Fosse's dance numbers.

Judy Holliday retired in 1960, after making *Bells Are Ringing*, and succumbed to cancer in 1965. In just a handful of feature films, she fashioned a unique twist on the dizzy blonde stereotype. As the simple-minded but sensitive innocent, she had the uncanny knack for speaking the truth in her quirky, piping voice.

1936-1959

Buddy Holly was popular with a wide audience. He appeared on television variety shows and was one of the first white acts to appear at Harlem's Apollo Theatre.

Looking at his thick glasses and boyish face in old publicity photos, Buddy Holly seems to be an unlikely rock star. But his hiccuping vocal style and ringing electric guitar heard on such all-time hits "Peggy Sue," "Rave On," and "Maybe Baby" are as fresh and exciting today as they were in the 1950s. Buddy's sound has been a major influence on the rock stars who have followed him into the limelight, including the Beatles, Eric Clapton, and Creedence Clearwater Revival. The great appeal of Buddy's music is that it speaks directly to his audience: teenagers. As one writer put it, "He was an Everyteen, mirroring the dreams and frustrations of anonymous small-town kids everywhere."

Charles Hardin "Buddy" Holley was born on September 7, 1936, in Lubbock, Texas. (He dropped the *E* from his last name after it was accidentally left off his first record contract.) Buddy was the youngest of four children in a conservative Baptist family. His parents were country music fans who encouraged him to learn to play the guitar, and as a kid he began to soak up the lonesome Western sounds he heard on the family's radio.

When he was barely into his teens, Buddy began singing in high school country music groups. Although it now seems almost laughably ironic, he once wrote in a sophomore composition class, "I have thought about making a career out of Western music if I am good enough, but I will just have to wait to see how that turns out."

By 1954 Buddy was beginning to make a name for himself, singing country music in small clubs in Lubbock and the surrounding area. Within a couple of years, the young singer had exchanged such country influences as Hank Williams, Jimmie Rodgers, and Bill Monroe for the more exciting sounds of rock 'n' roll played by Elvis Presley, Chuck Berry, and Little Richard.

Decca Records signed Buddy in 1956. He recorded several singles for the label in Nashville with his group, the Three Tunes, but he was quickly dropped when his music failed to make an impact. Returning home to lick his wounds, Buddy formed a new group, the Crickets, with guitarist Niki Sullivan, bassist Joe Mauldin, and drummer Jerry Allison. With the Crickets Buddy's unique musical style began to come together.

The group soon came under the wing of record producer Norman Petty, who owned a recording studio in Clovis, New Mexico. Petty used his connections to get "That'll Be the Day" picked up by Decca's Brunswick subsidiary. Once the record hit number one on September 14, 1957, the label signed Buddy and the Crickets as a group to one contract and Buddy Holly as a solo artist to another subsidiary, Coral Records. "They kicked us out the front door, so we went in the back door," joked Buddy. "That'll Be the Day" introduced Buddy's famous hiccuping style that became his signature. The hits came in quick succession with "Oh, Boy!" in 1957 and "Maybe Baby" and "Think It Over" in 1958. As a solo Buddy also recorded the 1957 megahit "Peggy Sue." Later, he recorded a sequel, "Peggy Sue Got Married."

The group took part in a number of cross-country tours with other recording artists, including Chuck Berry. He and Buddy liked to shoot craps in the back of the tour bus. Buddy was also friends with the flamboyant Little Richard. During one tour Buddy invited Richard to his home in Lubbock for dinner. At the time Lubbock was a conservative Southern town where racial segregation was the norm. When Buddy's father saw whom his son had brought home, he wouldn't let Richard in the door, but Buddy told his dad that if he didn't invite Richard to dinner, Buddy would never come home again. Richard joined the family for dinner, but they were not happy about it.

In 1957 the Crickets appeared on *The Ed Sullivan Show*, and they also toured England, making a big impact on the future of British rock music. Buddy's "brush and broom" picking style on his Fender Stratocaster electric guitar was scrutinized by such young guitarists as John Lennon and Eric Clapton.

Buddy eventually broke with both the Crickets and his producer Petty, and began to work as a solo artist. For his new backing group, Buddy assembled guitarist Tommy Allsup, drummer Charlie Bunch, and bassist Waylon

The Fender Stratocaster was an unknown commodity in the music world when Holly made it his instrument of choice in the mid 1950s.

Jennings, who would later go on to achieve great fame as a country singer. His last recording session took place on September 21, 1958, where he recorded "True Love Ways" and "It Doesn't Matter Anymore."

By 1959 Buddy was living in New York's Greenwich Village. The previous summer he had married Puerto Rican-born Maria Elena Santiago to whom he had proposed on their first date. He was also branching out musically, exploring pop styles and singing with orchestral backing. In the early winter of 1959, Buddy and his group took part in a cross-country tour with the Big Bopper (J.P. Richardson) and Mexican-American rocker Ritchie Valens. The musicians usually traveled by bus, but Buddy and his group decided to charter a private plane to take them from Mason City, Iowa, to Fargo, North Dakota, for their next show. At the last minute, the Big Bopper, who was ill, got Jennings to give up his seat, and Valens won a coin toss with Allsup for the other seat. Pilot Roger Peterson took off in a heavy snow storm on February 3, 1959, and crashed the plane. Everyone on board was killed, including 22-year-old Buddy Holly. His death stunned the music world. For one heartbroken fan, young Don McLean, it was "the day the music died," as he later put it in his 1971 hit "American Pie."

Brian Jones was an accomplished musician, who played clarinet, saxophone, and guitar. When he was first introduced to Mick Jagger and Keith Richard in 1962, Jones was sitting in with Britain's first real blues band, Alexis Korner's Blues Incorporated, at a small club in Ealing. Impressed by his talent, they invited him to join their new band. Jones came up with a name for the group, the Rolling Stones, which he based on a song by blues musician Muddy Waters.

Jones, who was born on February 28, 1942, grew up in a working-class community. His father was a factory worker and his mother taught piano. Jones had difficulty relating to his parents and spent most of his time listening to jazz records and dating. By the time he was 16, Brian had fathered two illegitimate children.

During the 1960s the Rolling Stones benefited from the phenomenal worldwide success of the Beatles. With their long hair and a street-wise attitude, the Stones were packaged as "the group parents love to hate." In 1963 the Stones released their first record, a cover of Chuck Berry's "Come On." In the summer of 1965, the Rolling Stones had a number-one hit: "Satisfaction."

That same summer, Jones began a tumultuous affair with Anita Pallenberg. Within a few weeks of meeting her, Jones abandoned his girlfriend Linda and their young son to move in with Pallenberg. She was also responsible for introducing Jones to LSD. Before long, scoring dope became Jones's number-one priority. Other members of the Stones also experimented with drugs. While Richard and Jagger were on trial for drug charges, the police raided Jones's apartment and charged him with possession of cocaine, Methedrine, and cannabis. All three Stones succeeded in having the charges against them dropped, but by 1969 Jones was so heavily addicted to heroin that his fellow band members felt they had no other choice but to fire him.

On July 3, 1969, Jones reportedly spent the evening guzzling vodka and swallowing downers. At midnight he decided to go swimming and dove into the pool. A few moments later, Brian Jones was discovered dead on the pool's bottom.

1942-1969

In 1964, when this photograph of Brian Jones was taken, the Stones released their first album, toured the United States for the first time, and topped the British charts for the first time with "It's All Over Now."

The original Rolling Stones were, from left to right, Bill Wyman, Brian Jones, Keith Richard, Mick Jagger, and Charlie Watts.

1943-1970

Always more hippie than hip,
Janis Joplin was moments
away from superstardom when
she tragically overdosed.

Janis Joplin was born in Port Arthur, Texas, on January 19, 1943. Her father worked for the Texaco Canning Company, and her mom had a job at the local college. Janis grew up in a comfortable middle-class home, but very little of the easy normalcy of her childhood home rubbed off on the restless young girl who was eager to get out and experience life.

At the age of 14, Janis became determined to be different from the other kids. She withdrew from her classmates whose tastes in music, clothes, and everything else she no longer shared. She read poetry, painted, and listened to folk music and the blues. Leadbelly and Bessie Smith were her favorites. Janis continued to live at home in Port Arthur until she was 17, when she finally struck out on her own.

Hanging out in Houston and Austin, Texas, Janis sang in honky-tonk saloons. Country-western music had never been her thing, but she found she could belt out a tune as well, if not better, than other country vocalists. After five years of singing and doing odd jobs, Janis had scraped together enough money to head out to San Francisco. She tried college but found that grooving on life was much more interesting and dropped out permanently after four attempts at higher education.

During 1965 Janis was singing regularly in folk and blues bars in San Francisco and Venice, California. Her voice had matured and she was beginning to develop her unique style. By this time Janis had already created the tough but vulnerable image of herself as a white blues mama. Even though she attracted some attention as a singer, she never made enough money and lived off unemployment checks. She went back to Austin in 1966 to sing with a country-western band, but Janis had not been there long before her friend Chet Helms told her about a new San Francisco band that was looking for a singer. Janis immediately returned to California and joined Big Brother and the Holding Company.

This time, everything came together for Janis. Big Brother allowed her to delve deeply into her pent-up emotions and express them through her folk and blues influences in a burst of dynamic energy. Her performances were explosive. As the band's popularity grew, Janis earned her reputation as the most powerful female voice in rock music.

Janis was a tough blues mama
on the outside, but when she
sang "Little Piece of My Heart,"
her vulnerability was made
painfully obvious.

Onstage with Big Brother and the Holding Company, Janis came alive with a raw energy that pulled her audience out of their seats.

In the summer of 1967, the Summer of Love, Janis was poised to blast to the heights of the rock scene. She found her launch pad at the Monterey International Pop Festival. Big Brother and the Holding Company stopped the show. Janis's performance was riveting. Her frenetic stage manner and thundering voice left the audience near hysteria. A star was born, and Albert Grossman, who managed Bob Dylan, became her agent and set out to make Janis a superstar.

Janis and the band made their first East Coast appearance at the Fillmore East in New York in February 1968. The press could not stop praising Janis, but there were few positive endorsements of Big Brother. This pattern was repeated almost every time the group appeared until the Holding Company finally broke up. After their second LP, *Cheap Thrills*, took off and Janis's single "Piece of My Heart" became a hit, she decided to split with the band and formed her own group.

Along with success in the music world came a slide into heavy drinking and drug use. Janis just could not seem to get her personal life together. Men came and went. She had affairs with women, but no one seemed to stay around long enough to give Janis what she wanted. She was almost always despairing over someone.

After splitting from Big Brother, Janis toured almost constantly. She was the television guest of Ed Sullivan, Dick Cavett, and Tom Jones. Even though she was quickly developing a heroin habit that compounded the physical devastation of her other abuses, Janis was achieving a level of fame that was way above the status of any other woman in rock music. In 1969 she released her first solo album. *I Got Dem Ol' Kozmic Blues Again Mama!* went gold. The diverse album includes songs by Rodgers and Hart, the Bee Gees, and Janis herself. She was back in the studio in the fall of 1970 to record *Pearl*, an album that she gave her own nickname. Her life seemed to be taking a turn for the better. Janis had a new band, Full Tilt Boogie, that she liked, and she was engaged to be married.

On October 4, 1970, it all came to an end. Janis Joplin was found in her room at Hollywood's Landmark Hotel, face down on the floor with needle marks on her arm. The coroner ruled her death an accidental heroin overdose. Janis didn't want a funeral. Her ashes were scattered and her friends gathered one last time for a big blast that was paid for by Janis's estate.

Pearl was released posthumously. The album went platinum. One track is the number-one hit version of Kris Kristofferson's song "Me and Bobby McGee," and another track, "Buried Alive in the Blues," is missing the vocals that Janis would have recorded had she lived.

▪ JOHN KENNEDY ▪

On May 29, 1917, Rose Fitzgerald Kennedy gave birth to the second of her nine children, John Fitzgerald Kennedy. His grandfather Patrick Kennedy was an East Boston saloon keeper who served six terms in the Massachusetts legislature and controlled the vote in East Boston. John's other grandfather, John Fitzgerald, became the mayor of Boston in 1910. Honey Fitz or the Little Napoleon, as he was called by friends and detractors, was a bundle of energy, blarney, and song, who charmed or riled everyone who crossed his path. When Joseph Kennedy married Honey Fitz's daughter Rose, two of Boston's most powerful political families merged.

John's father, Joseph P. Kennedy, was a taskmaster who had high expectations for his children. In his eyes politics was an esteemed profession, and he let it be known that he wanted at least one of his sons to become president of the United States. Although his older brother, Joe, seemed a natural for politics, John most often accompanied Honey Fitz on his rounds, listening to his speeches and his famed rendition of "Sweet Adeline." John was quiet but quick-witted, and he often amused his grandfather by mimicking his speeches.

In 1923, when John was six years old, Joe Kennedy moved his family from Brookline, Massachusetts, to Greenwich, Connecticut. John attended local private schools and then went to Choate, where he was better known for practical jokes than outstanding grades. At Choate he contracted double pneumonia. This kept him out of sports but gave him time to focus his attention on other things. In 1935 he graduated 64th in a class of 112, with no varsity letters, but he had the distinction of being voted most likely to succeed. His classmates were aware of qualities in John Kennedy that his high school record did not reveal. He was always able to say the right thing at the right time. He had a charming, self-deprecating sense of humor, but he was also tenacious and kept his word.

1917-1963

John Kennedy was often photographed in the Oval Office sitting in his Appalachian rocker, which gave him some relief from the back pain he constantly suffered.

In 1933 all the Kennedys, except Joe Junior, lined up for a family portrait: From left to right, they are Ted, Jean, Robert, Pat, Eunice, Kathleen, Rosemary, Jack, Rose, and Joseph P. Kennedy.

TOO YOUNG TO DIE 91

Unlike his brother Joe who obeyed his father's wishes by attending Harvard University, John chose Princeton. Joseph Senior agreed to this plan if John spent the summer studying at the London School of Economics. During the Atlantic crossing, he contracted jaundice and returned to Hyannis Port to convalesce. John went to Princeton that fall but had to withdraw because of his recurring illness. When he entered college a year later, John transferred to Harvard, graduating in 1940 with a degree in government.

Kennedy took post-graduate courses in business at Stanford University for six months before deciding to enter military service. He wanted very much to fight but had suffered a broken vertebra while playing junior-varsity football at Harvard and was a dubious prospect. John was unable to pass the Army physical and also failed to get into the Navy. In his determined way, he spent months doing strengthening exercises for his back until he was accepted by the Navy and assigned to work in the Pentagon. In 1941, after a year in Washington, he applied for combat duty. Late in 1942 Lieutenant Kennedy was sent to Portsmouth, New Hampshire, to complete torpedo boat training. Six months later he was in command of PT 109 with a crew of 10 men and two officers, based at Rondava in the Solomon Islands.

Under Kennedy's leadership, PT 109 carried out 30 attack and strafing missions without incident. On August 2, 1943, she was the lead ship on a night patrol when a Japanese destroyer rammed the boat in half, killing two of Kennedy's crew and injuring several others. Kennedy pulled his men together around the floating wreckage, knowing that if they could wait until dawn, he might be able to lead them to an unoccupied island three and a half miles away. The following morning, the sailors swam toward shore behind their commander, who pulled a badly injured crewman the entire distance. Several days later they were rescued. Kennedy was decorated for heroism and given the Purple Heart. He was then promoted to instructor at the PT boat school in Miami.

In 1944, with his spine injured again during the war, Kennedy entered the hospital in Hyannis to have a disk removed. His recovery was slow and torturous. While he was laid up, Joe was killed during a bombing mission over Belgium. Joe had talked of someday becoming president, and now Joseph Senior made it clear to John that he expected him to achieve this goal.

At the age of 28, John Kennedy entered politics. He returned to Boston to run for the eleventh congressional seat, which was the same Italian and Irish district that his grandfather Patrick Kennedy had once controlled. John fought hard and won. In Congress he promoted public housing for his dis-

This picture of 26-year-old Navy Lieutenant John Kennedy was taken on January 10, 1944, just after he returned to Los Angeles from duty in the Pacific.

New York turned out en masse to welcome John Kennedy with a ticker-tape parade.

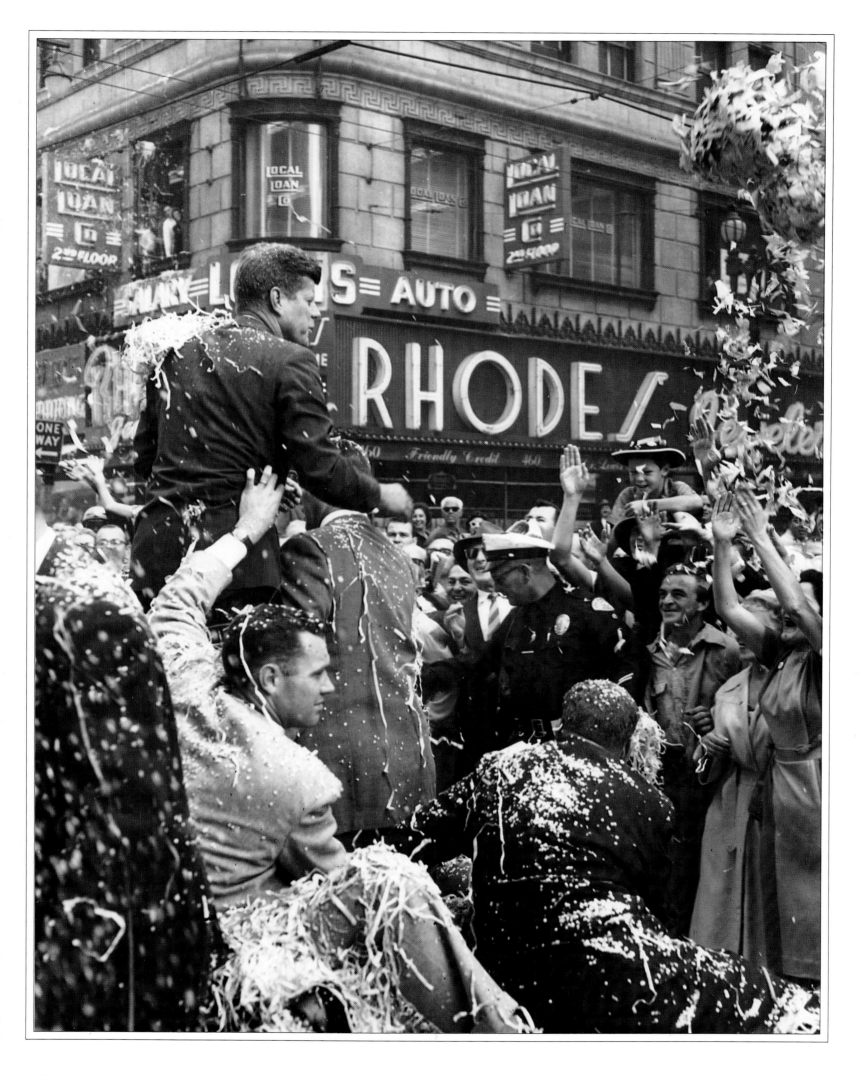

Kennedy met with Nikita Khrushchev in Vienna in June 1961. Following the summit, Khrushchev had the Berlin wall built and threatened to sign a separate peace treaty with East Germany. In a successful show of strength, the president called up the National Guard and the Russians backed away from the treaty.

Television made Americans equally familiar with the casual image of John Kennedy as a physically fit young father and the presidential image of a thoughtful world leader.

trict, and two years later, Kennedy won reelection by a five-to-one margin. In 1952, after completing his third term in Congress, John Kennedy announced that he would run for the United States Senate against Henry Cabot Lodge, who was a popular liberal Republican and had held his seat since 1936. His grandfather, the first Henry Cabot Lodge, had defeated Honey Fitz for the same Senate seat. The political experts did not give young Kennedy a chance.

The Kennedy family rallied to support John. His brother Robert became his campaign manager. John's sisters left their jobs and families to help, and his parents became active in the chase for votes. Public relations experts were hired. Advertising experts were hired. Kennedy money, influence, and backing were used at every step, and Massachusetts rang with Kennedy slogans. In the presidential election, Massachusetts went Republican for the first time in modern history, but John F. Kennedy defeated Henry Cabot Lodge by 30,000 votes.

Beginning his term in January 1953, Senator Kennedy espoused the same liberal causes that he had put forth as a congressman. He voted for public housing, a higher minimum wage, and the protection of the country's natural resources. In September John married Jacqueline Lee Bouvier, and the couple planned to live in a Virginia estate called Hickory Hill. Just after they moved into their new home, Kennedy's back problems worsened until he was forced to have a double fusion of his spine. The operation took place in October 1954, and he was still recovering in the spring of 1955. He ran his senate office from his bed and also found time to research and write a book about courageous men in American history. *Profiles in Courage* was published in 1956 and dedicated to his wife. It soon won the Pulitzer Prize for biography.

In the Senate, despite his time away, Kennedy was becoming an important figure. In 1956 he was asked to deliver the nominating speech for Adlai Stevenson. Even though Kennedy just missed the nomination for vice-president himself, he traveled widely for the Democratic ticket, giving 150 speeches in 26 states in five weeks. The party lost, but Kennedy seemed to gain. Many journalists remarked about the Kennedy smile, the Kennedy wit, the Kennedy charm, and the Kennedy courage. In 1958 he was reelected to the Senate by the widest margin of any candidate that year.

In October 1959 Kennedy invited 17 carefully selected men to a meeting in his Hyannis Port living room. They included his brothers, key members of his staff, his father, a public-opinion expert, a press-relations man, and the Kennedy in-laws. John spoke to them about the strategy for his presidential campaign. Robert Kennedy was again named his campaign chairman.

Kennedy announced his intention to become president of the United States on January 2, 1960. His strategy was to win the primary elections in carefully identified key states, beginning with Wisconsin. He immediately established his thorough and arduous style of working day and night, shaking as many hands as possible. After weeks of stumping in factories and small towns, he beat Senator Hubert Humphrey in Wisconsin by a small margin. In West Virginia Kennedy swept the primary, as he did in Indiana, Nebraska, Maryland, and Oregon. At the Democratic Convention in Los Ange-

John Kennedy, his wife, Jackie, and Vice-President Johnson prepare to greet state visitors to the White House.

les in 1960, Kennedy had formidable opponents in Lyndon Johnson and Hubert Humphrey, but the senator from Massachusetts beat them both. Then he named the second highest vote getter, Lyndon Johnson, as his running mate.

The campaign between John Fitzgerald Kennedy and Vice-President Richard Nixon was tense from the beginning. They were opposites in style and on the issues. While Nixon was stiff and earnest, Kennedy's easy smile and quickness emphasized his youth and charm. The turning point came when the two candidates appeared on live television for a series of debates. Kennedy's relaxed style won the day, and Nixon never fully recovered, although he lost the election by only 112,000 votes—the smallest percentage in American history.

John Kennedy was the youngest man to be inaugurated president. His term in office got off to a poor start when his anti-Castro invasion of Cuba failed. Later, a summit with Soviet Premier Nikita Khrushchev, on which President Kennedy had placed high hopes for world peace, was ineffectual. But in 1962, when the USSR attempted to move missiles into Cuba, Kennedy ordered a blockade. After five tense days, the Soviets gave in and agreed to remove their nuclear weapons from the region. On the domestic front, Kennedy attempted to actualize his campaign promise of a New Frontier, including increased federal aid to education, medical care for the aged, better housing laws, and new civil rights legislation. But Congress did not pass most of these measures.

In a special message to Congress in March 1962, President Kennedy proposed an eight-year program to acquire new federal lands for conservation and recreation. He asked for nine new national parks and for increases in the open spaces held by the states. He was committed to keeping mountains, plains, waterways, and forests as unspoiled as possible.

John Kennedy had wanted to be president and loved being president. His deep appreciation of the power and responsibility of the office showed in his bearing and action. By speaking of the possibilities for America, he had an ennobling effect on many American citizens. His presidency was alive with the spirit of youth and high resolve. The man who traveled to Dallas with his wife in late November 1963 was not only an accomplished legislator but a great inspirational leader whose best days seemed to be ahead of him. When he stepped into the back of a black limousine on November 22, he ordered the Secret Service to leave the cockpit open so he could make himself available to the crowd. The purpose of his trip was to heal a split in the Texas Democratic party before the 1964 presidential campaign. Texas Governor John B. Connally and his wife rode in jump seats near the Kennedys, and Vice-President Lyndon Johnson and his wife rode in a separate limousine behind the president's car.

At 12:30 P.M. the cars approached an expressway in Dallas for the last leg of the motorcade and drove past a seven-story building, the Texas Book Depository. Lee Harvey Oswald, a former Marine and an admitted Marxist who had once tried to become a Russian citizen, was at a sixth-floor window. He had an Italian rifle that he had bought from a mail-order company for $12.78, and he aimed it at the president's limousine. Witnesses heard three shots. The president was struck in the neck and head. Governor Connally was shot in the back. As the car sped toward nearby Parkland Hospital, Mrs. Kennedy cradled her husband's dying body, crying out for help. Doctors worked desperately to save the president's life, but he died without regaining consciousness.

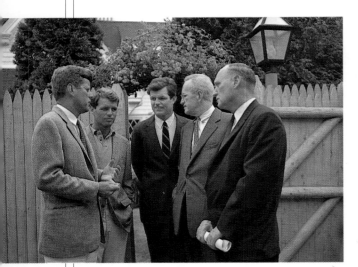

At the family's vacation compound in Hyannis Port, Massachusetts, the Kennedy brothers carry on with the business of government.

Jacqueline Kennedy, John-John, and Caroline attend the burial of John F. Kennedy in Arlington National Cemetery.

Robert Francis Kennedy was born in Brookline, Massachusetts, on November 20, 1925, eight years after the birth of his brother John. Because of their age difference, the two brothers grew up without much contact. John went off to prep school when Bobby was entering first grade.

A frail child whose weakness worried his mother, Bobby turned out to be the most openly aggressive and competitive Kennedy. As a little boy, he insisted on dressing like a sailor and broke several of his sisters' dolls. While his father said that Robert was the son most like himself, his mother appreciated his sincere religious beliefs. He served as an altar boy and considered becoming a priest. Bobby very much wanted to attend a Catholic prep school. His mother arranged for him to attend the St. Paul's School in New Hampshire, but when Bobby found out it was a Protestant school, he transferred to the Portsmouth Priory School, a Benedictine school in Rhode Island. His father insisted that Bobby attend a nondenominational prep school, and before the year was out, Bobby entered Milton Academy.

At Milton Bobby worked hard to get good grades and played football. During his senior year, in 1943, with his brother Joe flying bombing sorties in Europe and his brother John recuperating from his PT 109 injuries, Bobby insisted that he too should join the armed forces. He got his father's permission, and in March 1944 he reported to the Navy V-12 training school at Harvard. On the promise that he would see action if he accepted the rank of apprentice seaman, Bobby signed onto the U.S.S. *Joseph P. Kennedy, Jr.*, the ship named for his brother who had been killed in Europe. But his ship toured the Caribbean until the war ended.

In 1946 Bobby was discharged from the Navy and returned to Boston, where John was running for Congress. Family and friends had rallied to support his campaign. Joseph Kennedy turned to his 20-year-old son and asked him to campaign in the toughest and poorest section of East Cambridge, where the former mayor was expected to win five to one over all his opponents. If Bobby could cut that margin to four to one, it would be a great gain. Bobby started out ringing doorbells and speaking at spaghetti dinners, but one afternoon he saw some neighborhood children playing softball in a park near his office and decided to join them. They invited him back and soon the word got around that Kennedys were not too high class to play ball in East Cambridge. When the votes were in, John Kennedy was amazed to learn that half the votes cast in East Cambridge were for him.

The following year Bobby entered Harvard as a junior, after he and a friend had spent several months traveling in South America, where he was stunned by the abject poverty of so many people. He also became aware of the extent of poverty in America while working in tenement neighborhoods as a rent collector for Columbia Trust, a bank his father had once headed. After graduating from Harvard with mediocre grades, he was rejected by Harvard Law School but accepted late by the University of Virginia. To fill his time before he could start law school, Bobby got a job as a foreign corre-

1925-1968

Robert Kennedy was a visionary statesman who did much to advance the cause of civil rights, to end the tyranny of organized crime, and to make ending the war in Vietnam a mainstream issue.

Going back for a pass, Robert Kennedy comes close to being touch-tackled by his son during a family football game.

spondent for the *Boston Post* to report on the war between the Arabs and the newly created state of Israel.

Bobby started law school in the fall of 1948. He did not study hard, preferring to spend his time on community activities. He was elected class president and created the Law School Forum that brought nationally renowned speakers to the campus. At the end of his second year, Bobby married Ethel Skakel. She is a devout Catholic and became a friend to all the Kennedy sisters and her mother-in-law. Everyone agreed that the outgoing Ethel was the perfect match for Bobby.

After law school Bobby decided to become a $4,200-a-year attorney for the Internal Security Division of the Justice Department, but a few months later was transferred to the Criminal Division in Brooklyn, New York. His job was to investigate corrupt government officials, which he enjoyed, but when John asked him to manage his Senate campaign, Bobby left the Justice Department. He was 26 years old and not very experienced in politics, and he stepped on many people's toes. Bobby refused to honor the unspoken rules of conduct toward local political bosses and chose instead to reward campaign workers for their integrity and efficiency. To his credit the Kennedy campaign was one of the best-run political organizations in the country. When Bobby discovered that Massachusetts had many unregistered voters, his workers launched a major voter registration drive. On election day 70,000 new Democratic voters went to the polls, and his brother won the election.

Five years later, in 1956, John Kennedy again called his brother back from public service to help him become Adlai Stevenson's running mate for the upcoming presidential election. The fight was close, and even though Bobby stayed up all night attempting to swing delegates, too many stayed with Senator Estes Kefauver. Bobby gained further experience when he campaigned for Stevenson through the summer, working quietly in the background and filling notebooks with ideas about how to run a successful political campaign.

Many people were critical of President Kennedy's appointment of his brother as attorney general, but Bobby brought new status to the post, turning the Justice Department into an aggressive defender of civil rights.

Senator Kennedy and his wife, Ethel, were received warmly by the citizens of Alberta, Canada, during a good-will trip in 1966.

In 1957 Bobby became the executive director of the Senate's Labor Rackets Committee. With a staff of more than 100, Bobby was ruthless in prosecuting corruption in several major labor unions, especially the Teamsters. In 1959 he resigned to manage his brother's presidential campaign. During the race Bobby worked harder than anybody; some days he hardly slept and on one day he ran up a long-distance phone bill of $10,000. He again pushed hard for voter registration, bringing 5,000,000 Americans to the polls for the first time. On election eve in 1960, he arrived in Hyannis Port, thin, pale, and exhausted, but Bobby stayed up all night to hear the returns.

Between the election and the inauguration, John Kennedy decided to make his brother attorney general. At first Bobby refused, insisting that cries of nepotism would never stop. John said he didn't care. As always Bobby complied. As attorney general, he hired the best lawyers he could find. He wanted to create an aggressive team that could strengthen the rights of African Americans. He hired 40 black attorneys, and in 1963 he helped prepare the major civil rights bill that his brother sent to Congress. He also began work on legislation to establish free legal aid for poor people.

Robert Kennedy walks beside his brother's widow, Jacqueline Kennedy, at the president's funeral. Ted Kennedy is on Jackie's left and President Johnson walks behind other members of the family and Secret Service agents.

Robert Kennedy campaigned vigorously for the presidential nomination in 1968, and won five of the six primaries he entered.

After his brother's assassination, Bobby showed great courage at the funeral but a deep sadness soon overcame him. He had trouble working, relaxing, and even sleeping. He considered leaving government, but President Lyndon Johnson insisted that he stay on. He remained in his post until 1964, when he decided to run for the Senate from New York. Soon after renting a home on Long Island and with the Democratic party of New York overwhelmingly supporting him, Bobby began to travel through the state at his usual brisk pace. In November 1964 Kennedy easily won his Senate seat, as did his brother Teddy, who at 30 was the youngest person to be elected to the chamber.

From then on, the press assumed that Robert Kennedy would run for president. Bobby and Ethel were expecting the ninth of their 10 children, and his family entourage was often photographed. As the 1968 election approached, Kennedy vowed not to oppose President Johnson in the primaries, even though he was critical of many of his policies. When Johnson announced that he would not run, Kennedy threw his hat into the ring. Senator Eugene McCarthy had already surprised the nation by taking the New Hampshire primary. Kennedy knew that he would have to carry Indiana. He did win, but McCarthy took Oregon. This meant that the California primary scheduled for June 4, 1968, would be very important.

Kennedy conducted an exhausting campaign in California. He worked tenaciously for 14 hours a day, losing his voice and looking increasingly tired. On June 3 he came to the Ambassador Hotel in Los Angeles to rest. At midnight he spoke to a crowd of joyous campaign workers. The group was so enthusiastic that their candidate could not pass through the ballroom to exit. Instead, he was guided out through the kitchen. Sirhan Bishara Sirhan was waiting near a stairwell with a .22-caliber pistol. He shot and fatally wounded Robert Kennedy.

For Jack Kerouac the beat generation had a "sort of furtiveness with an inner knowledge that there is no use flaunting on that level, the level of the public, a kind of beatness, a weariness with all the forms, all the conventions."

Jack was born on March 12, 1922, and named Jean Louis. His parents were French Canadians. When Jean was five years old, his older brother Gerard died of rheumatic fever. Filled with guilt for just being alive, Jean took to the Catholic faith. He felt that he could never be free of sin and never become what his anti-intellectual father or his strong-willed mother wished him to be.

Jack changed his name when he started junior high in Lowell, Massachusetts. He played football and excelled in school. At his high school graduation, Jack announced that he was stopping his education to become a novelist. But his parents pushed him to accept a football scholarship from Columbia University. After two years, he dropped out and went to sea with the Merchant Marine.

Jack was soon back in New York City, where he would go wild and then write about everything he had done in graphic form. He had affairs with men and women, drank excessively, experimented with drugs, and did whatever he wanted to do whenever he wanted to do it. The men in his life were a loose group of friends who wrote and called themselves "New Vision." The group included Allen Ginsberg, William S. Burroughs, and David Kammerer.

In 1949 Jack finished his first novel, *The Town and the City*. It was accepted by Harcourt and Brace. That year Jack met Neal Cassady, his true partner, and together they began to travel the roads of America and explore the inner frontiers of their minds. Both men had a fearless preference for benzedrine. They also consumed enormous quantities of alcohol. At the beginning of the summer, Cassady would arrive at Kerouac's door, and they would set out for the open road. By October, which was Kerouac's self-appointed month of "breezy absolution and cleansing," he would return to his mother, wherever she happened to be, to hibernate and write until Neal knocked on his door the next year.

In April 1951 Jack began to type *On the Road* at 100 words per minute on pages of paper taped together into one long roll. Twenty days and 175,000 words later, he completed the novel, which tells about being lost in America with Neal. Viking finally published the book in 1957. Its success made Kerouac famous, and he filled his life brimful with drugs; homosexual adventures; affairs with women, including Neal Cassady's wife, Carolyn; explorations into Zen Buddhism; and writing.

Kerouac discovered that when he encountered a writer's block, the spoken word could be just as exciting as writing usually was for him. He began doing readings with musicians and booking talk shows. In 1960 Warner Brothers offered him $1,000,000 for the movie rights to *On the Road*, enhancing his popularity as a speaker. In his lectures Jack often spoke of the

1922-1969

During the 1960s, when this photograph was taken, Jack Kerouac was the self-appointed spokesman for the by-then defunct beat generation.

This photograph was taken during the late 1950s in New York. The woman behind Jack is Joyce Glassman, his on-again-off-again girlfriend of the time.

During World War II, Jack went to sea as a merchant seaman, but this yachting cap was just something Kerouac picked up on the road.

paradoxes of life. His poetic nature was soothing but confusing. He fascinated audiences, but many people left his lectures believing that Kerouac was crazy. He was suffering from vascular problems because of his overdoses of speed and had begun to drink more heavily. When he started to show up drunk for most of his speaking engagements, his career as a lecturer quickly went down the tubes.

Kerouac was floundering. He was a lonesome mystic, displaced in time and out of sync with American life. His drinking was constant, and he battled with delirium tremens. In the fall of 1961, he convalesced with his mother and wrote *Big Sur* in 10 days before returning to New York City. The following year he wrote *Visions of Gerard,* a sentimental memoir, which was not well received. For all his talk of inner peace, he actively and publicly supported the Vietnam War.

In 1969 Kerouac was living with Stella, his third wife; his mother; and his cats in St. Petersburg, Florida. He spent most days in front of the television. On October 21, 1969, Jack was watching *The Galloping Gourmet* and munching on a tuna sandwich, when his years of reckless self-abuse took their toll. A vein ruptured, hemorrhaging in his stomach. He called to his wife for help. By the time she reached him, he was in a fatal coma. Jack Kerouac died a few hours later; he was 47 years old.

For Martin Luther King Jr., the civil rights movement began one summer morning when he was six years old. Two of his friends did not show up to play ball, and Martin decided to go find them. He probably felt a little scared to leave his neighborhood to go to his friends' house several blocks away. The boys' mother met Martin at the door and told him that her sons would not be coming to play with him that day or any other day. They were white; he was black. Martin ran home crying. Years later, he admitted that those cruel words altered the direction of his life.

Martin Luther King Jr. was born on January 15, 1929. His father was a community leader and pastor of the Ebenezer Baptist Church in Atlanta, Georgia. His mother had been one of the first black women in Georgia to graduate from college and become a certified teacher. She filled the King home with books and taught Martin and his older sister to read long before they went to school. She also taught them about the politics of race and prejudice, explaining time after time that the end of slavery did not mean that blacks were truly free.

As a teenager, Martin sailed through school with great distinction. He skipped ninth and twelfth grades, and excelled on the violin and as a public speaker. One evening after taking the top prize at a debate tournament, Martin and his teacher were riding home on the bus, discussing the event, when the driver ordered them to give up their seats to two white passengers who had recently boarded. Martin was infuriated. "I intended to stay right in the seat," he recalled. But his teacher convinced him to obey the law, and they stood for the 90-mile trip. "That night will never leave my memory. It was the angriest I have ever been in my life."

Martin entered Morehouse College, his father's alma mater, when he was fifteen, planning to become a doctor or lawyer. He continued to be a brilliant student but also gained a reputation as one of Atlanta's best jitterbuggers. His friends nicknamed him Tweed for his stylish dress. After graduating from Morehouse, at the age of 19, he rethought his career plans and decided to enter Crozer Theological Seminary in Chester, Pennsylvania. This private nondenominational college had just 100 students, and only six were black. It was the first time that Martin had been in a community that was mostly white. He viewed the seminary as an opportunity to represent the cause of black scholarship and won the highest class ranking and a $1,200 fellowship for graduate school. In 1951 Martin entered Boston University School of Theology to pursue a Ph.D.

King's experience in Boston represented several milestones to him: He learned about urban life in a major northern city; he met and married his wife, Coretta Scott, who was a fine pianist studying at the New England Conservatory of Music; and he honed his philosophy of nonviolent resistance. While he was at Crozer, Martin had attended a lecture by Howard University president Mordecai Johnson, who spoke on Mohandas Gandhi, India's spiritual leader. Martin sat on the edge of his chair, listening to Johnson

1929-1968

In his last speech in Memphis, Dr. King said, "I don't know what will happen now, but it really doesn't matter to me. Because I've been to the mountaintop. . . . I may not get to the promised land with you, but I want you to know tonight that we as a people will."

Martin Luther King and Ralph Abernathy briefly visited London in 1964 to promote King's book *Why We Can't Wait*. He spoke hopefully of the progress the United States was making in civil rights and warned the British people to guard against race hatred.

On December 15, 1966, Dr. King testified before the Senate Government Operations Subcommittee in Washington, D.C.

Opposite:
On August 28, 1963, Martin was the last speaker to address the huge crowd of protesters that had gathered in front of the Lincoln Memorial to make the government aware of their support for pending civil rights legislation.

speak about the life and teachings of the man whose nonviolent protests had helped free his country from British rule. Gandhi's idea of Soul Force (the power of love, exercised through fasting, prayer, and demonstrating) gave Martin a basis for positive change. He arrived at Boston University determined to explore the philosophical underpinnings of nonviolent protest.

In 1954 Martin accepted a call to the Dexter Avenue Baptist Church in Montgomery, Alabama. Coretta had grown up in Alabama, where she witnessed her father's successful lumberyard burned down, set afire by jealous white merchants. It would be difficult for her to feel safe in racist Alabama, but she cautiously accepted her husband's choice.

Many local black ministers attended Martin's first sermon in his new church. Ralph Abernathy stepped forward after the service to congratulate Dr. King on his thought-provoking method of speaking. The two young Baptist ministers developed an immediate friendship, based on their shared understanding of the challenges of desegregating Alabama. Abernathy warned King that "Alabama would become the last state in the Union to accept desegregation." At first King doubted the native-Alabama preacher, but within a few months, he witnessed a dramatic example of Abernathy's pessimistic statement.

The incident that changed King's mind and altered the course of civil rights forever occurred on the cold night of December 1, 1955. Mrs. Rosa Parks, a seamstress who worked in a downtown Montgomery department store, boarded a bus for home, quietly paying and then sitting in the back. A few stops later, the driver ordered her to give her seat to a white man who was standing nearby. She politely refused. Montgomery bus drivers had a reputation of merciless treatment of Negro passengers, and the city's African-American leaders were looking for a way to challenge them. When Mrs. Parks refused to give up her seat, she was arrested, found guilty, and

In 1956 Martin Luther King addressed the convention of the National Association for the Advancement of Colored People, NAACP, in San Francisco.

fined $10. When her attorney received the verdict, he announced to the court that his client would appeal.

In response to Rosa Parks's courage, the town's black leaders formed the Montgomery Improvement Association and elected Martin Luther King its president. The immediate goal of the MIA was to boycott the city's buses until the public transportation laws were changed. Martin Luther King set the tone of the boycott with an often quoted speech: "In our protest," he said in slow cadences, "there will be no cross burnings. No white person will be taken from his home by a hooded Negro mob and brutally murdered . . . We must hear the words of Jesus echoing across the centuries: Love your enemies, bless them that curse you, and pray for them that despitefully use you."

The Montgomery strike was long, bitter, and violent. When the downtown merchants began to complain to city officials that their businesses were suffering, the city responded by pressing charges against King and Abernathy for interfering with the stores' operations. While King was attending a circuit court trial to appeal the charges, he was handed a message on a folded note. The United States Supreme Court had affirmed the decision by the Alabama Supreme Court that local laws requiring segregation on buses were unconstitutional. It was over. The first major civil rights battle had been won. But for King, whose home had been firebombed and looted, it was only the first of many battles.

On November 29, 1959, Martin offered his resignation to the members of the Dexter Avenue Baptist Church. Speaking to the congregation

Martin was always eager to meet with students to encourage them to complete their educations and to become involved in the struggle for their civil rights.

Receiving the Noble Peace Prize in 1964 galvanized Martin to continue speaking out on civil rights and poverty in America.

for the last time he said, "I have come to the conclusion that I can't stop now . . . I have no choice but to free you." Months earlier he had been elected president of a new organization dedicated to resolving injustice, called the Southern Christian Leadership Conference (SCLC). There was no longer time to lead a church.

King moved his family to Atlanta, where he began to establish a regional network of nonviolent organizations. As an adjunct to SCLC, students formed the Student Nonviolent Coordinating Committee (SNCC). In April 1961 King coordinated SCLC, SNCC, and other advocates of desegregation to take two bus loads of white and black volunteers through the South on a "freedom ride." The intention of the tour was to attempt to integrate strategically chosen, segregated lunch counters and rest rooms. In Virginia and the Carolinas, no one was harmed, but in Alabama the freedom ride became a rolling horror that many people witnessed on television. In Anniston, Alabama, one bus was burned and its passengers were beaten with pipes and chains. In Birmingham angry mobs greeted the bus with more violence. Many of the riders had to be hospitalized. The violence shook Martin, and he wanted to abandon the risky freedom rides before one of the passengers was killed. But students from SNCC defied King and insisted that the bus drive to Montgomery. There they and an observer from the Kennedy administration were brutally beaten.

In January 1963 the month King arrived in Birmingham, George Wallace was sworn in as governor, vowing that Alabama would never be integrated. King and Ralph Abernathy organized a freedom march. The city

Martin's parents sit behind his
four children and their close
friends at Dr. King's funeral.

filed an injunction against them, prohibiting their gathering. The marchers ignored the injunction. Wholesale arrests were followed by an outcry of support for the marchers. Three months later, another march was planned with the intent of "turning the other cheek" to the violence of the city's police force. Children as young as six were among the marchers. As they reached Birmingham's downtown, police and firemen terrified the crowd with high-pressure water hoses and police dogs. Hundreds of the protesters were arrested. The following day, more marchers repeated the walk, which led to more arrests. On the third day, King organized still another march to the city jail, which was now teeming with more than 1,200 protesters, who were locked in small, hot cells, singing "We Shall Overcome." As King approached the jail, the chief of police warned them that his forces would attack. The marchers were undaunted. The police chief ordered his men to attack but nothing happened. He then ordered the fire fighters to turn on their hoses. They also refused. Instead, the men, some with tears streaming down their faces, parted their lines to let the protesters through.

The nonviolent strategy had succeeded. The merchants of Birmingham called for immediate negotiations. After meeting with King and local African-American leaders, they agreed to hire black clerks and integrate lunch counters, fitting rooms, and drinking fountains within 90 days.

Following the victory in Birmingham, Martin Luther King called for a rally in front of the Lincoln Memorial in Washington, D.C. On August 28, 1963, nearly 200,000 people stood in the intense heat listening to the speakers. By the time King came to the podium as the day's final speaker, the crowd was hot and tired. He had prepared his speech for weeks, hoping to define a new direction for peace. As he mounted the steps to the podium, he put his notes aside and decided to speak from his heart. He spoke of freedoms granted and not yet achieved. He then spoke the words that continue to echo throughout the world: "I say to you today, my friends, that in spite of the difficulties and frustrations of the moment, I still have a dream. It is a dream deeply rooted in the American dream. I have a dream that one day this nation will rise up and live out the true meaning of its creed, We hold these truths to be self-evident that all men are created equal. I have a dream."

By mid October 1964, Martin had given 350 civil rights speeches and traveled 275,000 miles. His workday had been 20 hours long for 13 years. He had reached a point of total exhaustion and had just checked into an Atlanta hospital when his wife brought him the telegram announcing that he had won the Nobel Peace Prize. After a brief rest, he went back to work.

In the spring of 1968, King traveled throughout the country, speaking about the need to bring people together in a more unified, peaceful way. In April he stopped in Memphis to meet with two of his advisors, James Bevel and Jesse Jackson, to discuss organizing a poor people's march on Washington. At five-thirty on the evening of April 4, King walked onto the balcony of the Lorraine Motel to speak with Andrew Young. As he stepped through the door, he saw Jesse Jackson and yelled to him to join them for dinner. Jackson agreed, and as King paused, a shot split the air. Martin Luther King fell to the floor.

With his bushy mustache and eyebrows and ever-present cigar, comedian Ernie Kovacs was an unusual prime-time television star even in the 1950s. Using an appealing combination of slapstick humor and a hip surrealistic sensibility, he pioneered a style of television comedy on his network programs that heavily influenced such shows as *Saturday Night Live* and *Late Night with David Letterman*.

Ernie was born in Trenton, New Jersey, on January 23, 1919. As a child he became interested in acting. He starred as the Pirate King in his high school's production of *The Pirates of Penzance*. After high school Ernie attended the New York School of the Theatre. From 1936 to 1939, he acted in stock theatre companies on Long Island. He eventually formed his own stock company, but it failed when he was hospitalized for 19 months with pleurisy and pneumonia.

Even as a young man, Ernie was developing a reputation as something of a renaissance man. He wrote a column for a Trenton newspaper, worked as a disc jockey, created jokes for nightclub comedians, and dubbed voices for cartoons. But the new medium of television appealed most to him. Ernie began his television career as the host of a daytime cooking show on Philadelphia's WPTZ, and later he hosted a combination quiz and talk show.

In 1951 NBC-TV took a chance on Ernie and gave him his own summer replacement series, *Ernie in Kovacsland*. One critic described the show as "wild and casual, witty and foolish, and clever and idiotic." For the next six years, Ernie hosted a series of shows for NBC, CBS, and the DuMont network, including *The Ernie Kovacs Show* and *Kovacs on the Corner*.

Ernie was a master of the blackout sketch. One of his shows might treat viewers to four or five minutes of a man sucking up spaghetti to the tune of Beethoven's Fifth or of a woman enjoying a bubble bath while a procession of midgets emerges from beneath the suds. He became famous for such characters as the lisping poet Percy Dovetonsils and the Nairobi Trio—three well-dressed musical apes who took turns bopping each other over the head in time with the music.

Ernie had a truly off-center sense of humor. He once told a friend, "In the beginning, the network, the sponsor, and all my friends said, 'We dig you, Ernie, but nobody else will.' Now, I get cabdrivers who say, 'I dig you, Ernie, but you oughta see the guys I get in this cab!'"

In 1954 Ernie married Edie Adams, a glamorous singer and actress who appeared on many of his television shows. In 1957 Ernie achieved a number of firsts: He played his first straight dramatic role in a television adaptation of *Topaze*; he published a critically acclaimed novel, *Zoomar*; and he appeared as a stiff-necked Army captain in the movie *Operation Mad Ball*. That year he also appeared as a character who had some of the qualities of Charlie Chaplin in a half-hour special for NBC, which featured no dialogue. No wonder *Time* magazine called Ernie "one of television's few fresh and lasting performers."

1919-1962

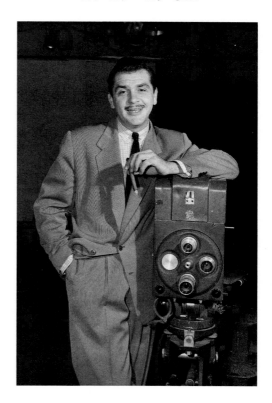

Ernie Kovacs was one of the most inventive comedians on television during the 1950s. His humor was almost entirely visual, and although it seemed offbeat, it was accessible to a large audience.

Edith Adams sang on *Ernie in Kovacsland* during the summer of 1951. She later married the show's star and shortened her name to Edie.

Regular comedy features on Kovacs's television shows included "Mr. Question Man," "You Asked to See It," "Percy Dovetonsils," "The Nairobi Trio," and "Clowdy Faire, Your Weather Girl."

Toward the end of the 1950s, Ernie was busy with movie and television projects. He and Edie moved from New York to Beverly Hills, where Ernie shared his workroom with a burro that occasionally chewed up scripts when he left the room. In 1961 he wrote, directed, and starred in several half-hour specials, and in the fall he began a new series of monthly prime-time specials for ABC, *The Ernie Kovacs Show*.

Driving home from a baby shower at the home of Milton Berle on January 13, 1962, Ernie's car skidded on a rain-slick Los Angeles street and broadsided a utility pole. His death at 42 ended a career that had brought laughter and joy to millions of television viewers.

▪ BRUCE LEE ▪

Nearly 20 years after Bruce Lee's death was announced, a tribe of bushmen in Malaysia still believe that the film star is alive. They are convinced his reported death on July 20, 1973, was an outlandish publicity stunt for the movie he was shooting, *The Game of Death*. One day, Bruce will return from the dead to star in a series of new kung fu pictures. In the meantime, along with millions of other Bruce Lee fans worldwide, they are content to sit through repeated viewings of his old movies.

Bruce Lee was born in San Francisco on November 27, 1940. On the night of his birth, his father was 3,000 miles away in New York's Chinatown performing comedy on the stage of the Cantonese Opera, a Chinese vaudeville theatre. Lee's mother, Grace, named him Lee Yuen Kam, which means "protector of San Francisco." One of the nurses decided that the baby needed an American name and dubbed him Bruce Lee.

When Bruce was three months old, his family returned to Hong Kong. Thanks to his father's show-business connections, Bruce starred in 20 films while he was a teenager, using the name Lee Siu Loong. By the time he was 13 years old, he had become a serious student of martial arts. To his parents' dismay, he often got into violent street fights, using techniques he learned from his martial arts classes. Concerned that Bruce was developing into a dangerous punk, his parents sent him to live with relatives in the United States when he turned 18, temporarily halting Lee's movie career.

Eventually, Bruce ended up in Seattle, where he enrolled at the University of Washington. He continued to study martial arts and worked with an instructor who had the unlikely name of Yip Man. Bruce earned his living working as a waiter at a Chinese restaurant. In 1964 he married another martial arts student, Linda Emery. Shortly after their marriage, the couple moved to Oakland, California, and soon Bruce opened a martial arts school. To promote the venture, he gave demonstrations at local tournaments. Hairdresser-to-the-stars Jay Sebring saw Bruce at a tournament in Long Beach and recommended him to producer William Dozier, who was looking for a Chinese-American actor to costar in his new television series, *The Green Hornet*. Dozier obtained films of Bruce in action and quickly signed him to a contract.

Bruce appeared in 30 episodes of *The Green Hornet*. Later, he guest starred on several television shows and had a featured role in the movie *Marlowe*. To supplement his income between acting assignments, Bruce taught private martial arts lessons to some of Hollywood's most prominent movie stars, including Steve McQueen, James Garner, and James Coburn.

In 1971 Bruce returned to Hong Kong, where he filmed a low-budget feature, *Fists of Fury*. He was paid $7,500. *Fists of Fury* became Hong Kong's all-time top-grossing feature, and when it was released in America, Bruce immediately became an international star. Three more films followed, culminating in *Enter the Dragon*, Bruce's first starring role in a Hollywood production.

1940-1973

Bruce Lee was in his mid 20s when he costarred on *The Green Hornet*, but he had already made 20 movies in Hong Kong while he was a teenager.

Bruce Lee began to train seriously in Kung-Fu in Seattle. His master, Yip Man, taught him that the art was not only a means of self-defense but also a way of life.

On July 20, 1973, Bruce went to visit actress Betty Ting Pei in her Hong Kong apartment to discuss a role for her in one of his upcoming movies. When he complained of a headache, Betty offered him a prescription painkiller called Equagesic. While he was waiting for the medication to take effect, Bruce rested in Betty's bedroom. A short while later, she tried unsuccessfully to wake him and phoned for an ambulance. Within the hour, Bruce was rushed to a nearby hospital, where he was pronounced dead. The coroner ruled that Bruce had suffered a fatal reaction to the painkiller.

Shortly after his death, *Return of the Dragon*, the third martial arts film Bruce Lee made in Hong Kong, was released in America. The ads for the movie voiced a sentiment felt by Bruce Lee's millions of fans: "Boy, do we need him now."

From an angry young working-class lad in Liverpool, England, to the peace-espousing spokesman for a generation to a doting New York house-husband, John Lennon has presented many faces to the world. The lasting legacy of his music, his words, and his actions conveys the memory of an honorable man who did his best to make the world a better place to live. Even people who disagree with his viewpoints and methods respect his integrity.

John Winston Lennon was born on October 9, 1940, in Liverpool during a German air raid. His father, Fred Lennon, was a steward on troop ships. He rarely saw his young son and left his wife Julia in 1942. John spent most of his childhood living with Julia's strict but loving sister Mimi and his uncle George. The childless couple doted on their nephew and raised him as a son in their comfortable home in a suburb of Liverpool. John was a bright child, but he was mischievous. He visited Julia as often as he could. She lived with her parents not far from Aunt Mimi's house. Julia inspired John's interest in music, teaching him a few banjo chords on a guitar that his aunt had reluctantly bought him. Mimi didn't think much of John's aspirations to be a musician. Many times she cautioned him, "The guitar's all right as a hobby, John, but you'll never earn a living from it."

Inspired by the folk, or skiffle, craze that was sweeping Britain in the mid 1950s, John formed his first group, the Quarrymen. But the music that really captured his imagination was rock 'n' roll. He listed to early records by Elvis Presley, Buddy Holly, and Little Richard. John once said that after hearing Elvis's "Heartbreak Hotel" for the first time, "Nothing was ever the same for me."

In the summer of 1957, John met 15-year-old Paul McCartney from neighboring Allerton while the Quarrymen were playing at a church fair. At the time Paul was a better musician than John, who immediately drafted him into his group. Later that year, when John began his studies at the Liv-

1940-1980

In 1964 John Lennon was the leader and driving force behind the Beatles.

John was photographed in West Germany in 1960. The ghostly figure in the background is the Beatles' bass player, Stuart Sutcliffe, who died of a brain tumor in 1962 at the age of 21.

The Beatles' collarless Pierre Cardin suits were a far cry from the scruffy look John had cultivated before the band signed with Brian Epstein.

erpool College of Art, he would often get together at lunchtime to play guitar and sing current rock 'n' roll hits with Paul and his friend George Harrison. They were both students at a high school around the corner from the art college. George soon joined the group as well.

In July tragedy struck. Julia, with whom John was spending more and more time, died after she was run over by a car. His mother's death when he was only 17 haunted John for most of his life, inspiring such songs as "Julia" and "My Mummy's Dead." The tragedy also brought him closer to Paul, whose own mother had died two years earlier.

By 1960 the group had settled on the Beatles as their name and were working steadily in clubs around Liverpool. With a new drummer, Pete Best, the Beatles booked an extended gig at a club in the infamous red-light district of Hamburg, West Germany. There John's anarchic humor ran rampant. He regularly gave the audience mock Nazi salutes, and one night John played an entire show with a toilet seat around his neck.

When the Beatles returned to Liverpool, they began making regular lunchtime appearances at a basement club called the Cavern. Brian Epstein first heard the group there and offered to manage them. Although John's cruel sense of humor was often directed at Brian, who was both a homosexual and a Jew, he eventually grew closer to their manager than any of the other Beatles.

By 1962 the Beatles were one of northern England's biggest draws. When Brian secured a recording contract for them with EMI, they hired their old friend Ringo Starr to replace Best on the drums. John and Paul had become a gifted songwriting team, with John's raw rock 'n' roll sound nicely complementing Paul's more pop-oriented melodic sense. In August John married his art-school sweetheart Cynthia Powell. She was pregnant with their son Julian, who was born the following April.

Beatlemania enveloped England in 1963, but no amount of success could stop John's irreverent sense of humor. Asked to perform at the prestigious Royal Variety Show, which was attended by the Queen Mother and Princess Margaret, he quipped from the stage, "Will the people in the cheaper seats clap your hands? All the rest of you can just rattle your jewelry."

By early 1964 Beatlemania was also sweeping the United States. At one time Beatles records held the top five positions on the pop singles chart. John was beginning have severe problems coping with living his life in the public eye, and he especially detested the show-biz aspects of the music business. To relieve his anxiety and maintain his own voice, John wrote poetry and nonsense prose. When a collection of his writing was published as *In His Own Write*, it hit the British best-seller lists.

The differences between John and Paul became more noticeable with the coming years. By 1965 most of the songs written under the umbrella of Lennon-McCartney were actually written separately. That year, in honor of their incredible success, the Beatles were made Members of the British Empire by the queen. Showing his usual disdain for authority, John smoked marijuana in a Buckingham Palace bathroom before the ceremony. Five years later, he returned his M.B.E. medal to protest Britain's support of the Vietnam War.

At the peak of his Beatles years, John's father came back into his life. He actually showed up on John's doorstep in 1966. John harbored a great deal of resentment toward his father for deserting him and Julia, but he bought his father a house and made sure he received a weekly check to cover his living expenses. Sick of touring and playing to crowds whose screams drowned out their music, the Beatles retired from the road at the end of the year. John's view on this: "Beatles concerts are nothing to do with music any more. They're just bloody tribal rites."

John enjoyed the wealth that being a pop star brought him. He had a home with a swimming pool in the "stockbroker belt" and an art nouveau Rolls Royce. But he was increasingly feeling the need to be more than just a pop singer. Always a man with firm convictions, he began to speak out on issues. To make his views on war perfectly clear, he appeared in an antiwar movie, *How I Won the War*. In 1966, after he met a kindred spirit, Yoko Ono, at a showing of her avant-garde conceptual artwork, a new John Lennon began to evolve. As John's affair with Yoko became increasingly less discreet, she introduced him to an arty crowd in London that reminded him of his happy

John and Cynthia attend the British premiere of *The Knack, and How to Get It* in 1965. John had initially been attracted by Cynthia's reserved manner and blonde good looks, but drifted apart from her when his interests strayed to politics and mysticism.

Until 1967 John was rarely photographed wearing glasses, so this picture, probably from 1965 or 1966, may be from a rehearsal.

Late 1968 brought John's most
hirsute look yet. Here, the
tastemaker for a generation of
young people looks almost
antiquarian.

John, Yoko, Kyoko (Yoko's
daughter), and Julian (John's
son) enjoyed a Scottish holiday
in July 1969. Later during this
same vacation, the Lennons'
car crashed in Sutherland,
Scotland. No one was hurt, but
all were kept overnight in a
hospital for observation.

Opposite:
By early 1969, when *Let It
Be* was recorded, the Beatles
were no longer a cohesive unit.
John had already recorded an
avant-garde solo album with
Yoko and was eager to
branch out further.

art school days in Liverpool. While Yoko was taking John in a new direction and his marriage to Cynthia was ending, the Beatles were releasing their landmark of psychedelia, *Sgt. Pepper's Lonely Hearts Club Band*.

Drifting further and further away from the other Beatles, John began to collaborate on experimental projects with Yoko. The album cover of *Two Virgins* shows John and Yoko naked front and back and caused a storm of controversy. John and Yoko were true soul mates, and their romance has become one of the great all-time love stories. "I've had two partners in my life, Paul McCartney and Yoko," John once said. "That's not a bad record, is it?"

By late 1969 the Beatles were finished as a group. John and Yoko put together the fictitious Plastic Ono Band, and John recorded his first solo hit, "Give Peace a Chance." After legally changing his middle name to Ono, John married Yoko. To celebrate their union, they participated in a series of highly publicized "bed-ins" for peace.

John's childhood insecurities and pain surfaced with a vengeance on his first solo album, recorded in 1970. Under the tutelage of psychologist Arthur Janov, whose book *The Primal Scream* was his bible for a time, John sang such intensely personal songs as "God," "Mother," and "My Mummy's Dead." Feeling free from some of his emotional baggage left over from both the Beatles and his childhood, John moved with Yoko to New York in 1971.

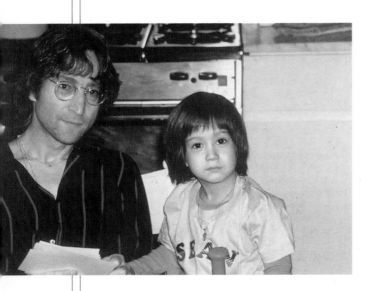

Following a well-publicized estrangement from Yoko during 1973-74, John redirected his energies to hearth and home following the birth of his son Sean in 1975.

Almost immediately they fell in with such well-known counterculture figures as Abbie Hoffman and Jerry Rubin. Those associations and their antiwar efforts resulted in the Lennons being tailed constantly by the FBI. They were denied permanent residency by the United States government, but they went on living in New York. In 1976 John finally won his fight to remain in America.

In late 1973 the fairy-tale romance between John and Yoko began to sour. Their spending virtually 24 hours a day together for the last seven years had taken its toll. Yoko's solution was for John to move out and go about sowing whatever wild oats he still needed to sow. For a 15-month "lost weekend," John staggered through bars and nightclubs in Los Angeles and New York with his rock star pals, including Ringo, Keith Moon, and Harry Nilsson. Prophetically, one of the songs on his *Walls and Bridges* album, which was released during this period, was "Nobody Loves You (When You're Down and Out)."

Although they stayed in touch by phone, John and Yoko did not see each other again until they met at an Elton John concert in late 1974. John was remorseful and begged Yoko to take him back. She invited him to move back into their sumptuous apartment in the Dakota, an apartment building overlooking Central Park. Yoko had suffered at least two miscarriages, and the Lennons were delighted to learn that Yoko was expecting again. On John's 35th birthday, October 9, 1975, Yoko gave birth to their son, Sean. His birth transformed John into a househusband. He handled all the domestic chores of raising Sean for the next five years while Yoko oversaw their many business interests.

As the 1970s turned into the 1980s, John quietly began to return to the limelight. He had been inspired to write several new songs while he was vacationing in Bermuda, and in August 1980 he and Yoko went into a New York studio to record what would be his comeback album, *Double Fantasy*. Featuring such odes to ordinary life and his love for Yoko as "Watching the Wheels," "(Just Like) Starting Over," and "Woman," the album rocketed to the top of the charts when it was released in November. After five years out of the media's eye, John and Yoko began popping up everywhere, doing interviews on radio, TV, and newspapers, and breaking their long silence. "Life begins at 40—or so they say," John told an interviewer. "It's like I'm 21 again and saying, 'Wow, what's gonna happen now?'"

In December John and Yoko were back in the studio working on a follow-up to *Double Fantasy*. Returning home on the evening of December 8, as he and Yoko neared the entrance to the Dakota, John turned when he heard a voice call his name. An emotionally unstable fan, Mark David Chapman, fired five shots at John Lennon's back. He died shortly after at the hospital.

A few days later, all over the world, fans held silent vigils in John's memory. In New York's Central Park, across from the Dakota, nearly 400,000 fans turned up to pay their respects. The voice of a generation may have been silenced, but his spirit would never die.

During much of her Hollywood career, blonde bombshell Carole Lombard was probably better known for her famous Hollywood husbands—William Powell and Clark Gable—than for her own sparkling work. Today, movie critics and fans recognize her as a gifted film comedienne. Her work in pioneering screwball comedies, such as *Twentieth Century*, *My Man Godfrey*, and *To Be or Not to Be*, continue to delight viewers.

Carole was born Jane Peters in Fort Wayne, Indiana, on October 6, 1908. Her parents divorced while she was still a child, and she moved to Los Angeles with her mother. Like many stars, Carole's movie career began as a fluke. According to legend, 13-year-old Carole was playing baseball in her backyard when she caught the eye of director Allan Dwan, who immediately signed her for a small role in his 1921 movie, *A Perfect Crime*.

After taking acting and dancing lessons, Carole was signed by the Fox film company and secured starring roles in *Marriage in Transit* and *Hearts and Spurs*, before an automobile accident resulted in the studio canceling her contract. Two years later she joined Mack Sennett's studio and appeared in many of the comedic shorts for which that production company was famous.

In the late 1920s Carole was best known as a good-looking blonde with great legs, who looked terrific in a slinky evening gown. She had no trouble attracting the attention of several of Hollywood's best-known leading men. In 1931 Carole married actor William Powell, but after two years they divorced.

While she was under contract to Paramount Pictures, Carole's stylish work in such movies as *Fast and Loose*, *It Pays to Advertise*, and *Man of the World* began to show Hollywood's star makers that she was more than just

1908-1942

Carole Lombard was a radiant beauty and an accomplished actress, who knew how to be truly funny when she wanted to be.

Carole Lombard gives John Barrymore what he has coming to him in a compartment on the famous New York-to-Chicago train in this scene from the movie *Twentieth Century*.

Carole's performance in *Made for Each Other* changed her screen image, bringing her much-deserved recognition as a dramatic actress. This photograph was made in the late 1930s about the time that movie was released.

Even on the 20-acre ranch that Lombard and Gable owned in the San Fernando Valley, Carole was often photographed elegantly dressed.

another pretty face. In 1932 she starred with her future husband Clark Gable in *No Man of Her Own*. It was the only film the two ever made together.

In 1934, when director Howard Hawks cast Carole for *Twentieth Century*, opposite John Barrymore, her new image was created. In the movie she played a starlet who was discovered by talent scout Barrymore. He chases her across the country on the train named in the movie's title. The film is the first screwball comedy, and in it Carole shaped a character that was as sexy as she was funny.

Her role in the whimsical farce *My Man Godfrey*, with her ex-husband Powell, netted Carole an Academy Award nomination for best actress in 1936. By the following year, Carole was Hollywood's highest-paid actress, earning close to $500,000. Her work during the late 1930s impressed one critic so much he remarked that "only the need for a dark-haired heroine kept her from getting the Scarlett O'Hara role in *Gone With the Wind*." It was a role that she badly wanted, since she and the movie's male lead, Clark Gable, had been married in 1939.

While Carole made her name in comedies, she also turned in exceptional performances with serious roles in such movies as *Made for Each Other*, with Jimmy Stewart, and Alfred Hitchcock's tale of marital misadventure, *Mr. and Mrs. Smith*, with Robert Montgomery. But Carole Lombard is perhaps best remembered for her last movie role. Along with radio star Jack Benny, she starred in director Ernst Lubitsch's anti-Nazi comedy set in Poland, *To Be or Not to Be*.

Returning from appearances at a series of war bond drives, Carole died in a plane crash near Las Vegas on January 16, 1942. Her death at age 33 stunned America and her husband never really recovered from her loss. President Franklin D. Roosevelt sent his condolences to Gable in a telegram that in part reads, "She brought great joy to all who knew her and to millions who knew her only as a great artist. She is and always will be a star, one we shall never forget nor cease to be grateful to."

Hollywood journalists used to joke that Jayne Mansfield became a movie star just so she could go to the opening of a drugstore or supermarket and be photographed. Her self-promotion antics during the Broadway run of the play *Will Success Spoil Rock Hunter?* are legendary. Show time was eight o'clock, and like the rest of the cast, Jayne was required to be at the theater by seven-thirty. Since she was often being photographed with other celebrities at a movie premiere, Jayne would rush to the theater only seconds before the curtain rose. The absurdity of a stage actress attending movie premieres at the same time she was expected to perform onstage never occurred to Jayne. What mattered to her was getting her picture in the paper.

She was born Vera Jane Palmer in Bryn Mawr, Pennsylvania, on April 19, 1933. She was raised in Phillipsburg, New Jersey, and Dallas, Texas, where she met her first husband, Paul Mansfield. They married when she was 16 years old. After Jayne graduated from high school, the newly married couple enrolled at Southern Methodist University. Later, they moved to Los Angeles, where Jayne hoped to break into movies.

In 1955 Jayne was *Playboy*'s February Playmate. When she was sent to Florida to promote the Jane Russell movie *Underwater*, Jayne managed to attract more attention than the movie's star. Playwright George Axelrod saw a picture of Jayne and immediately cast her in his new play, *Will Success Spoil Rock Hunter?* When the play was adapted for the screen in 1957, Jayne reprised her role. She also starred in *The Girl Can't Help It*, a lively music-filled comedy also written by Axelrod. Later, she starred in *The Wayward Bus* and *Kiss Them for Me*. Unfortunately, Jayne's talent for acting was not as big as her skill for winning publicity, and she soon found herself demoted to small parts in Hollywood movies, although she continued to star in European productions. Despite her loss in stature, Jayne lived like a star in a huge pink mansion on Sunset Boulevard that once belonged to singer Rudy Valee. Since pink was her favorite color, she decorated the house in pink and white. She also built a heart-shaped swimming pool. To pay the bills, Jayne developed a live musical-comedy stage act, which she premiered in Las Vegas. Later, she took the act on the road.

While she was married to Paul Mansfield, Jayne had her first child, Jaynie Marie, on November 8, 1950. Her marriage to Mansfield ended in 1956. A year later, she married Mickey Hargitay, a nightclub performer and onetime Mr. Universe. They had three children, Mickey Jr., Zoltan, and Mariska, before divorcing in 1963. In 1964 Jayne married producer-director Matt Cimber, and they had a son, Antonio. In 1966 Jayne divorced Cimber. She then became involved with her divorce attorney, Sam Brody. Their affair prompted Brody's wife to initiate a divorce suit against him. Mrs. Brody charged that during their 10 years of marriage her husband had been unfaithful to her with 40 women. But Jayne was the only woman she named.

In late June 1967 Jayne traveled to Biloxi, Mississippi, where she performed her act at a small nightclub. She was accompanied by Brody and her three children from her marriage to Hargitay. Following her last perfor-

1933-1967

Jayne Mansfield's fabulous figure brought her fame, but she was also an intelligent and gifted actress who never appeared in public out of character.

Joan Blondell, Jayne Mansfield, and a friend crowd into a berth for a bedtime chat in this scene from *Will Success Spoil Rock Hunter?*

three children from her marriage to Hargitay. Following her last performance in Biloxi, on June 29, Jayne and her entourage headed for New Orleans, where she was scheduled make a television appearance. Ronnie Harrison, a 20-year old law student at the University of Mississippi, was driving them in his 1966 Buick. Just outside New Orleans, a crew was spraying insecticide into the air to kill mosquitos. The driver of a huge truck-trailer rig had difficulty steering his vehicle through the mist and slowed down. On the same stretch of highway, Harrison's car sped around a curve and hit the rear of the trailer. The force of the collision ripped the top off the car instantly killing the three adult passengers in the front seat. Jayne's three children were rushed to a New Orleans hospital, where they survived with minor injuries.

Few artists in this century have been as loved and as hated as Robert Mapplethorpe. He was born on November 4, 1946, in Floral Park in Queens, New York. His father was an electrical engineer and amateur photographer. A devout Roman Catholic, he and Robert's mother insisted that their six children attend parochial school.

Mapplethorpe began looking for ways to change the world around him while he was still in school. He rebelled against his parents and their religious beliefs. His clothes, his art, and his manner of expression were energetic, singular, and offbeat. Robert lived in a traditional lower-middle-class neighborhood, but he was attracted to Manhattan and began to hang out in the city while he was a teenager. He was drawn to the galleries and the city's bizarre array of people. Robert Mapplethorpe also had a quieter side. His mother loved to garden, and he enjoyed helping her tend her flowers.

In high school Mapplethorpe was already defining himself as an artist. He leaned toward abstract art, spurning photography because it interested his father and was too dull and representational for his flamboyant tastes. In 1963, when Robert graduated from high school, he submitted a portfolio of his work to the Pratt Institute and was accepted. Once he was living in Manhattan, Mapplethorpe went wild, experimenting with many kinds of sexual expression. It took him six years to graduate from Pratt, and during that period he never took a picture. In his final year of college, Robert decided to make collages of cutouts from pornographic magazines. His work was considered outlandish and remarkable.

At about the time he left Pratt, Mapplethorpe met a wealthy art collector, Sam Wagstaff. He was 20 years older than Robert, but the two formed a lasting relationship. In 1971 Mapplethorpe convinced Wagstaff to visit a collector in Syracuse, New York, who had a large charcoal drawing of two men in an erotic embrace by Tom Findland. The picture turned out to be only a print, but the same collector also happened to have a series of photographs

1946-1989

The controversy engendered by recent showings of Robert Mapplethorpe's photographs has made the name of this talented New York artist a household word.

Straightforward portraiture that allows the subject to project his own image is a trademark of Mapplethorpe's work.

At the Institute of Contemporary Art in Boston in July 1990, staff workers Scott Blum (left) and Vincent Marasa (right) hang a photo from Mapplethorpe's *Ajitto* series.

The range of subject matter Mapplethorpe photographed is much broader than many of his critics, who are often totally unfamiliar with his work, realize.

of young men engaged in sexual activities. Mapplethorpe convinced Wagstaff to buy the photos. Later, with Mapplethorpe's help, Wagstaff became one of New York's premier photo collectors. Robert Mapplethorpe, with Wagstaff's support, became one of the country's leading photographers.

As his collages evolved, Mapplethorpe began taking Polaroid pictures of friends to use in his art. Soon, he found that controlling his own photography worked to his advantage. People who saw his early photos admired their sensitivity to tone and shape. In 1976 Mapplethorpe had a solo exhibition of his work at New York's prestigious Light Gallery.

From Polaroids to prints, Mapplethorpe soon found a form of expression that fitted his artistic sensibilities. He loved black-and-white photography, particularly portraits, and became an outstanding printmaker. By the late 1970s, his work had taken two different directions: His portraits were beginning to be published in fashion magazines around the world, while his sexually bizarre images were frequently displayed in galleries and museums. In 1983 the Robert Miller Gallery began to represent Mapplethorpe, cataloging his controversial photos, his portraits, and his beautiful flower pictures for exhibition and sale.

Mapplethorpe's life was as extraordinary as many of his images. His homosexual excesses became legendary, partly because of his explicit photos and also because he openly admitted to participating in them. In 1986 he was diagnosed as having AIDS. He suffered from the symptoms of the disease for the next three years, but during this period of time, he produced some of his most stunning prints.

By 1989 Robert Mapplethorpe was terribly weakened by his disease. He died on March 9. During his lifetime eight books about his work had been published, and he had started the Robert Mapplethorpe Foundation to fund AIDS research as well as photo exhibitions. When Mapplethorpe died, he was only 42 years old. His foundation and the remarkably diverse body of his black-and-white photographs continue to thrive.

After growing up poor in a Jamaican slum, Bob Marley went on to become not only reggae's most famous musician, but also a figure revered throughout the word for the political and social activism he urged in his music. His group, the Wailers, had a major impact on the direction of rock music in the 1970s. Such major stars as Eric Clapton, Paul Simon, and the Rolling Stones recorded his songs or otherwise sang his praises.

Robert Nesta Marley was born in the village of St. Ann, Jamaica, on February 6, 1945. His father was a British Army captain, Norval Marley, whose wife, Cedella, was only 17 years old when Bob was born. The marriage broke up when Bob was eight, and he and his mother moved to a house in Kingston's Trench Town slum area. Cedella did domestic work to earn enough money to send Bob to private schools.

The Marleys shared their home with the Livingston family. Bob formed a series of singing groups with his best friend Bunny Livingston and another friend Peter Tosh. The group finally settled on the Wailing Wailers as a name. Eventually shortening their name to the Wailers, the group had its first hit in 1964 with "Simmer Down," a song Bob wrote as a warning to rowdy Jamaican youths.

After a brief stay in the United States to be with his mother, who was living in Delaware, Bob returned to Jamaica, where he fell in with the Rastafarian religious sect. Rastas worship the Ethiopian emperor Haile Selassie as a god and draw inspiration from Marcus Garvey's Back to Africa movement. Bob grew his hair in long dreadlocks and started singing about Rastafarian beliefs.

The Wailers' first album was *Catch a Fire*. Released in 1973, its songs decry the evils of Trench Town and the harassing tactics of the Jamaican Army, and promote Rastafarianism. The Wailers' mixture of hypnotic reggae rhythms with serious subject matter influenced rock acts, including the Rolling Stones and Linda Ronstadt, to add elements of reggae to their music. In 1974 Eric Clapton had a major hit with a note-perfect version of Bob's "I Shot the Sheriff."

The Wailers began to tour the world in the mid 1970s, helping to turn reggae from an indigenous Jamaican style of music into an internationally appreciated sound. In 1974 Livingston and Tosh left the group for solo careers after recording *Natty Dread,* but the Wailers continued with Bob as the undisputed star.

On December 3, 1976, gunmen broke into Bob's Kingston house where he and his group were rehearsing for a Smile Jamaica concert sponsored by the Jamaican government. Bob and his wife, Rita, were wounded in the cross fire. A few days later a triumphant Bob Marley appeared in front of 80,000 fans at the concert, showing the world that even a politically motivated attempt on his life could not slow him down.

A string of successful albums, including *Rastaman Vibration* and *Babylon by Bus*, brought the Wailers into the late 1970s. In 1979 Bob was given

1945-1981

In the years since his death, Bob Marley's popularity and powerful influence on other musicians has grown even stronger than it was during his lifetime.

Bob Marley's music captures the full scope of the Jamaican experience in a range of lyrics that express everything from romantic love to left-wing political principles.

a citation by the United Nations for his work on behalf of Third World nations. In April of the following year, the newly created African nation of Zimbabwe (formerly Rhodesia) invited Bob to the state-sponsored independence day ceremonies. Bob called this "the greatest honor of my life."

After collapsing onstage at a Wailers concert in Pittsburgh in the fall of 1980, Bob entered New York's Sloan-Kettering Hospital for cancer treatments. He later transferred to an experimental clinic in West Germany. On his way back to Jamaica to receive the Order of Merit from Prime Minister Edward Seaga, Bob was hospitalized at the Cedars of Lebanon Hospital in Miami. He died there in his sleep on May 11, 1981, from the combined effects of lung, liver, and brain cancer. He was 36 years old.

Jamaica gave Bob Marley a state funeral 10 days later. It was attended by 100,000 people, including the prime minister.

Christa McAuliffe

Until July 1985, 37-year-old Sharon Christa Corrigan McAuliffe led an ordinary life. She was a wife and the mother of two young children. During the day she taught at a high school in Concord, New Hampshire. Then NASA announced that her application to join a space shuttle crew had been accepted. Christa was astounded that she had made it to the final cut. People who knew her understood why. A school official in Concord explained, "To us, she seemed average. But she turned out to be remarkable. She handled success so beautifully."

When Christa appeared on television talk shows and news programs, viewers were usually left with one significant impression: She seemed so down to earth. Christa was the eldest of five children. She grew up in Framingham, Massachusetts, where she attended a Roman Catholic high school. She was a B student, and she participated in several extracurricular activities, sang in the glee club, and played both volleyball and softball. During her high school years, Christa met her future husband, Steven. After graduating from Framingham State College, they married in 1970 and moved to Washington, D.C., where Steven earned a law degree from Georgetown University. While he was attending law school, Christa worked on her master's degree in education at Bowie State College in Maryland. Later, they moved to New Hampshire, where Steven joined the staff of the state's attorney general.

When she learned she was pregnant, Christa immediately began keeping a daily journal in a spiral notebook. A typical entry included a report about her doctor's appointment, news of friends, and the cute things her cats had done. "This was my history for my children," she explained. "I would have loved to know my mother's life that way." Besides teaching full time, Christa led a Girl Scout troop, volunteered at a daycare center, and raised money for the local hospital.

1948-1986

Christa McAuliffe and other members of the Challenger crew stride confidently toward the space shuttle on the morning of the fateful launch.

At home in Concord, New Hampshire, Christa posed for a family portrait with her husband Steven and their children, Scott and Caroline.

Christa joined the Challenger crew that already included Francis R. Scobee, Michael J. Smith, Ronald E. McNair, Ellison S. Onizuka, Judith A. Resnik, and Gregory B. Jarvis.

Christa was a warm, outgoing person who enjoyed the fun and the hard work of being an astronaut. Here, she rides in a parade with her children, Caroline and Scott.

Students at Concord High looked forward to the classes Christa taught. She designed her courses to present the practical aspects of the law and to give a clear view of the positive role American women have played in history. She wanted everyone, including herself, to have a chance to do their best. "What are we doing here? We're reaching for the stars," she said soon after joining the astronaut program. Realizing her celebrity would be temporary, Christa looked forward to returning to Concord. After several months of training, she missed her family as well as her students.

On Tuesday morning, January 28, 1986, at Cape Canaveral, Florida, the Challenger space shuttle prepared to launch. Adverse weather conditions had already canceled the Challenger's trip on four different occasions. Christa's parents, Grace and Ed Corrigan, along with Christa's two children, Scott and Caroline, were at Cape Canaveral to witness the launch. Scott's third-grade class had also flown in from Concord. Christa's students gathered in Concord High's auditorium to watch it on television. As the Challenger lifted off, the crowd cheered. Only 70 seconds later, their mood abruptly changed to quiet disbelief. The Challenger had suddenly exploded. Among the spectators, Ed Corrigan was the first to absorb the impact of what had just happened. Instinctively, he placed an arm around his wife. Grace Corrigan's look of bewilderment dissolved into tears as she rested her head against her husband's shoulder.

That evening, President Ronald Reagan was scheduled to give his annual State of the Union address. It was postponed for a week. Instead, the president appeared on television to address the day's tragedy. In a poignant tribute to the Challenger's crew, the president said, "They had a hunger to explore the universe and discover its truths. They wished to serve, and they did—they served all of us."

Speaking before an audience several months earlier, Christa commented on the journey she was about to make. She said simply, "I touch the future. I teach."

Singer Clyde McPhatter lives on whenever his pure tenor voice is heard on the Drifters' classic "White Christmas" or his solo hit "A Lover's Question."

Clyde was born on November 15, 1932, in Durham, North Carolina. His father was a Baptist preacher, and his mother played the church's organ. Clyde grew up singing gospel music. During the 1940s his family moved to New Jersey, where Clyde kept singing. He started several gospel groups while he was in high school. After graduation Clyde worked briefly as a clerk, but he also sang with groups in New Jersey and Harlem.

In 1950 17-year-old Clyde joined Billy Ward's Dominoes as the lead vocalist. Ward's group formed an important link between gospel music and rhythm and blues, which was essentially gospel music with the word *Baby* substituted for the word *Lord*. Clyde sang on the Dominoes' hits "Have Mercy Baby" and "The Bells." Eventually, he grew tired of Ward bossing him around and making him pay fines for such offenses as wearing unshined shoes. Clyde quit the Dominoes in 1953 to form his own group with the backing of Atlantic Records' president Ahmet Ertegun.

Clyde's new group became the Drifters, and they recorded many hits including "Money Honey" and "Such a Night" before Clyde was drafted into the Army in 1954. When his stint in the service was completed in 1956, McPhatter decided to launch a solo career. His biggest hits were "A Lover's Question" in 1958 and "Lover Please" in 1962. By the early 1960s, pop music tastes were changing and teen idols were the rage. Even though Clyde was just reaching 30, he was an old man in the record business. His string of hits had come to an end, but his emotion-charged singing style continued to influence such singers as Ben E. King and Smokey Robinson. Clyde never gave up his dream of breaking out of the rhythm-and-blues category into mainstream show business alongside Perry Como and Nat "King" Cole.

He never realized his dream. When he was only 39 years old, Clyde McPhatter was found dead in the dressing room of a nightclub where he was performing. It was June 13, 1972, and Clyde had died from complications of heart, liver, and kidney disease.

1932-1972

Clyde McPhatter was the first lead singer for the Drifters. He recorded only six records with the group before he was drafted in late 1954.

1904-1944

Glenn Miller and his swing band recorded several big hits, including "In the Mood," " Little Brown Jug," "Sunrise Serenade," and Glenn's theme song, "Moonlight Serenade."

Glenn Miller was born in Clarinda, Iowa, on March 1, 1904. When he was five years old, his family moved to Nebraska. Glenn was 13 years old when he purchased his first instrument: a trombone. He earned the money by milking cows for two dollars a week. John Mossbarger, who sold Glenn the trombone, sensed the boy's keen interest in music and encouraged him to learn the fundamentals. The following year Glenn's family moved to Fort Morgan, Colorado. In high school there, Glenn studied music and played football.

Shortly after graduation in 1921, Glenn landed his first professional job with the Boyd Senter orchestra. He played with the band for a year before enrolling at the University of Colorado to study music. In 1923 Glenn left college to be a full-time musician. He moved to Los Angeles, where he played with Max Fisher and Georgie Stoll. Soon, Ben Pollack invited Glenn to play with his band, which included such accomplished musicians as Benny Goodman and Gil Rodin, at the Venice Ballroom. When Pollack's band left for Chicago, Glenn accompanied them. He was still with them in 1928 when they arrived in New York.

Ever since he left Colorado, Glenn had maintained a long-distance romance with Helen Burger, who had also been a student at the university. On October 6, 1928, they married. Their marriage prompted Glenn to settle down in New York, where he was able to study arranging with Joseph Schillinger. He resigned from Pollack's band and managed to find enough work to support himself as a free-lance trombonist and arranger.

By 1932 Glenn had started playing with the Smith Bellew Orchestra. When it disbanded in Denver in early 1934, Glenn returned to New York, where he joined the newly formed Dorsey Brothers band. A year later, he left their band to assist Ray Noble in organizing his first American orchestra. Throughout much of the 1930s, Miller also worked as a sideman and arranger for other bands. He was saving his money in hope of forming a band of his own. "I was tired of arguing about arrangements, of having things come out different from the way I wrote them," he told an interviewer. "I wanted actually to hear my ideas and I figured the only way I could was with my own band." Glenn's desire to launch a band was so strong that he passed on the $350-a-week position MGM offered him.

Glenn Miller plays trombone with his orchestra during a live broadcast from a hotel ballroom in 1940.

Glenn Miller's Orchestra finally became a reality in 1937. Unfortunately, his drummer Maurice Purtill left him for another band the first night his band played at the Hotel New Yorker. In the subsequent months, the band endured many growing pains as Glenn tried to achieve a suitable sound. That same year, Helen was also battling a serious illness. Compounding matters, Glenn's finances were bleak.

By January 1938 Glenn had suspended his band. In a late-night discussion with his wife, he toyed with the idea of returning to free-lance work. Helen, who had absolute confidence in her husband's talent, encouraged him not to make any drastic decisions. The following spring, Glenn reorganized his band. Besides a handful of holdovers from the earlier group, he hired several new members. Si Shribman, who owned half a dozen prestigious ballrooms on the East Coast, had confidence in Glenn and frequently booked his band. In September Glenn Miller's Orchestra added an attractive singer, Marion Hutton.

To keep his band afloat, Glenn often booked the group for one-night stands. One night in early 1939, while the band was making its way through a blizzard, the bus stalled. A farmer graciously invited the band to take shelter in the warmth of his kitchen until morning, when they were able to get the bus started again. For Glenn it was a night of reflection. Looking back on the difficult times his band had experienced, he decided the struggle was worth it. "Taking the bad breaks teaches you to stay together," he commented later. "After that, we weren't just a band—we felt like a band."

By summer Glenn Miller and his orchestra were playing to sold-out houses in New York. Two of his recordings, "In the Mood" and "Tuxedo Junction," were topping the charts. In 1941 Glenn and his band were performing three shows a week on national radio. When a reporter questioned Glenn about his tremendous success, he responded, "It's an inspiring sight to look down from the balcony on the heads of 7,000 people swaying on the dance floor—especially when you are getting $600 for every thousand of them." That year, Glenn earned his first million.

Success had a positive effect on Glenn's demeanor. When he had been preoccupied with making his dream happen, friends nicknamed him Gloomy Glenn. After only a few months on the bandstand with his own orchestra, Glenn learned to smile. He seemed really to enjoy giving people the kind of music they wanted to hear.

In 1942 Glenn registered for the draft. Later that year, he became a captain in the United States Army and was appointed director of bands for the Army Air Force Technical Training Command. In 1944 he was stationed in England. Every Saturday morning, Glenn and his band of musical servicemen performed on the radio. In December Glenn and his band were told to leave for Paris. Glenn departed ahead of the others to make arrangements. "He left before we did—as he usually did," commented band member Peanuts Hucko. "He didn't leave it to anybody; he didn't send out a scout. He was a scout." En route to Paris on December 15, his plane mysteriously disappeared. No trace of it was ever discovered. A year later, Glenn Miller was declared officially dead and awarded a posthumous Bronze Star.

In 1942 Glenn Miller disbanded his popular dance band to join the Army, where he led a large orchestra that broadcast regularly from England to troops stationed throughout Europe and Africa.

The first time Sal Mineo had a switchblade pulled on him he was in the fourth grade. This was exactly the kind of violent scene his parents tried to escape when they moved to the Bronx from Harlem. Unfortunately, by the time Sal, who was born on January 10, 1939, reached grade school, the neighborhood had deteriorated. To help their son realize there was another way to live, his parents sent Sal to acting classes. When he was 11, a theatrical producer visited his class and picked him for a small role in Tennessee Williams's play *The Rose Tattoo*.

In 1952 Sal received critical acclaim for his performance as the crown prince in the Broadway production of *The King and I*. After two years in the play, Sal appeared in his first movie, *Six Bridges to Cross*. A year later, he co-starred in *The Private War of Major Benson*. In 1955 he was cast in a movie that would earn him an Oscar nomination for best supporting actor: *Rebel Without a Cause*. Sal was also nominated for an Emmy for his performance in *Dino* on *Studio One*. In the late 1950s Sal recorded several pop songs. "Start Movin'" sold more than a million copies. In 1960 he received a second Oscar nomination for best supporting actor for his performance in *Exodus*.

By the late 1960s Sal was disillusioned with his life in Hollywood. He sold his big house and decided to concentrate on projects that would bring him personal fulfillment. He was particularly interested in producing a screen version of Charles Graham's novel *McCaffrey*. Sal also acted in and directed plays, most notably *Fortune in Men's Eyes*.

On February 12, 1976, Sal had his second encounter with a switchblade. Following a rehearsal for the play *P.S., Your Cat Is Dead*, Sal headed home to his apartment in West Hollywood. In the building's basement garage, he was confronted by a man wielding a knife. Neighbors heard screams and found Sal lying in a pool of blood. Within minutes Sal Mineo was dead.

Ironically, that same day William Belasco, his producing partner, had finalized a deal with a major studio to start production on *McCaffrey*. A memorial service for Sal was scheduled to be held at Belasco's home. It never took place. The night before the service, Belasco was killed in an automobile accident.

1939-1976

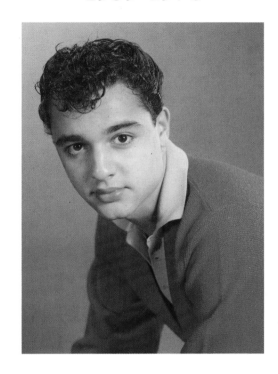

In 1959, when this photograph was taken, Sal Mineo was a popular young actor on stage, scene, and television.

In John Ford's 1964 epic *Cheyenne Autumn*, Mineo played a young man who joins his people in a harrowing attempt to leave their Oklahoma reservation to return to their original home in Wyoming.

1926-1962

This studio portrait of Marilyn Monroe was taken in 1953 while she was working for 20th Century-Fox. She wore the same dress in the photograph on the cover of the premier issue of *Playboy*.

Sexy dumb blonde—these three words come quickly to many peoples' minds when they think of Marilyn Monroe. She was the sex symbol of the 1950s, but the qualities that made Marilyn Monroe an international movie star also kept her from proving she could be more than just another pretty face. No one was more aware of this than Marilyn herself. When she greeted her public, she was all smiles, but in the privacy of her home, Marilyn was a bundle of insecurities. Despite the adoration of millions of fans, she felt misunderstood and fretted that she was nothing but a loser.

She was born Norma Jeane Baker on June 1, 1926, in Los Angeles General Hospital, conceived out of wedlock to Gladys Monroe Baker. Her father was probably C. Stanley Gifford, who had worked with Gladys at Consolidated Film Industries in Hollywood. Gladys eventually relinquished her daughter to the care of state-operated foster homes. The young Norma Jeane escaped the loneliness of her childhood by daydreaming. "I dreamed of myself becoming so beautiful that people would turn to look at me when I passed," she said.

When she was 16 years old, Norma married 22-year-old Jim Dougherty. In 1944 he joined the merchant marine, and she moved in with her in-laws. She spent her days working in a defense plant, inspecting parachutes. A sharp-eyed photographer from *Yank* magazine spotted Marilyn while visiting the factory and asked her to pose for him. It was the beginning of her career as a photographer's model.

Marilyn registered with the Blue Book Model Agency, where she learned how to apply makeup. Following the advice of an agent, she also dyed her brown hair blonde. The transformation had an incredible effect on the way men perceived Marilyn. When she walked down the street, they made no secret of their attraction toward her. Marilyn's modeling assignments led to pictures of her appearing on the covers of several national magazines. It also led to the dissolution of her marriage to Dougherty.

In 1946 Marilyn completed a successful screen test at 20th Century-Fox and was offered a $75-a-month contract. Shortly after signing the contract, she traded in her drab, humble-sounding name for the more glamorous Marilyn Monroe. Her career at Fox got off to a slow start. She landed bit parts in two movies, *Scudda Hoo! Scudda Hay!* and *Dangerous Years*, but her performance in the first ended up on the cutting-room floor and she went unnoticed in the second. In 1947 Fox executives let their contract with

With her brown, kinky hair straightened and dyed blond, Norma Jeane's modeling career took off in 1946 when she began to pose as a pinup for *Laff, Peek, See, Glamorous Models, Cheesecake,* and *U.S. Camera.*

In the movie *Some Like It Hot* Marilyn played Sugar Kane, a kooky singer with an all-girl orchestra, who befriends two new girl musicians played by Tony Curtis and Jack Lemmon.

Marilyn entertained more than 100,000 troops in Korea. The temperature was bitter cold, but after 10 shows Marilyn said that she felt only the warmth of the adoring soldiers.

Marilyn lapse, complaining that she was not photogenic enough to become a movie star.

To pay the bills, Marilyn returned to modeling, but she continued building connections in the movie industry. Joe Schenck, a 70-year-old producer who was a cofounder of 20th Century-Fox, turned out to be a powerful ally. He used his influence to help Marilyn win a contract with Columbia Pictures. In 1948 Marilyn costarred in a low-budget musical *Ladies of the Chorus*, but executives at Columbia felt her performance lacked sparkle and unceremoniously dropped her option after six months. Marilyn resumed modeling. When a photographer approached her about posing nude for a pinup calendar, she reluctantly accepted.

A short while later, Marilyn found work in a Marx Brothers' comedy, *Love Happy*. Executives at United Artists enthusiastically hailed her performance as "Mae West, Theda Bara, and Bo Peep, all rolled into one" and immediately sent her on a national tour to promote the movie. Johnny Hyde, a Hollywood talent agent, saw Marilyn in *Love Happy* and was convinced she could become a star. Marilyn turned her career over to Hyde and followed his recommendation to have plastic surgery on her nose and jaw.

Hyde used his influence to win Marilyn small roles in two major Hollywood movies, *The Asphalt Jungle* and *All About Eve*. Marilyn's relationship with Hyde became complicated when he asked the young starlet to marry him. Marilyn refused. Despite the rejection, he continued to be her biggest supporter. Unknown to Marilyn, Hyde suffered from a serious illness. Months before his death, he won his client a seven-year contract with 20th Century-Fox at $750 a week.

Marilyn's return to Fox led to minor roles in several movies produced between 1950 and 1952. In early 1952 she completed *Clash by Night*, produced by RKO. Weeks before the movie's scheduled release, executives at RKO discovered the calendar featuring a nude Marilyn. Rather than deny the model's identity, the executives cannily arranged to have information about the calendar leaked to gossip columnists with quotes from Marilyn claiming she posed for the photographs because she was flat broke. By the time *Clash by Night* opened, Marilyn Monroe was a household name. The notoriety she received inspired theater owners to place her name first on marquees.

Marilyn's career suddenly took off with starring roles in *Don't Bother to Knock*, with Richard Widmark; *Niagara*, with Joseph Cotten; and *Gentlemen Prefer Blondes*, with Jane Russell. Then she starred with Lauren Bacall and Betty Grable in *How to Marry a Millionaire*. These pictures were box office bonanzas, earning millions of dollars for the studio, but Marilyn was only being paid $1,200 a week. When she wanted to negotiate a new contract, the studio turned her down. When she refused to appear in *The Girl in Pink Tights* because she was unhappy with both the script and her role in the picture, Marilyn was placed on suspension.

In 1954 Marilyn married Joe DiMaggio, the beloved Yankee Clipper, after a stormy two-year courtship. DiMaggio believed a wife's place was in the home and wanted Marilyn to give up her career. As a farewell to her pub-

Playing three ambitious women determined to marry millionaires, Marilyn, Betty Grable, and Lauren Bacall showcased their considerable talents in this 1953 movie.

lic, Marilyn interrupted her honeymoon to entertain troops in Korea. She then returned with DiMaggio to his lavish home in San Francisco. The life of a housewife did not suit Marilyn, and she yearned to resume her career. When the studio approached her about starring in *There's No Business Like Show Business*, Marilyn readily accepted the offer. The movie flopped, and Marilyn's marriage to DiMaggio disintegrated.

In 1955 Marilyn's career rebounded with a starring role in *The Seven Year Itch*. The picture's success improved her position in Hollywood, but Marilyn's personal life suffered. She and DiMaggio decided to separate, and Marilyn traveled to New York, where she began studying with Lee Strasberg, the founder of the Actors Studio. Lee's wife, Paula, took Marilyn under her wing and became her personal acting coach. While she was studying at the Actors Studio, Marilyn fell in love with playwright Arthur Miller. Anxious to marry Marilyn, Miller initiated divorce proceedings against his first wife. Marilyn, whose divorce from DiMaggio was already final, began studying Judaism, intending to convert after the marriage.

In early 1956 Marilyn was finally given the opportunity to show her dramatic talent in *Bus Stop*. After completing the picture, she and Miller married in June. They honeymooned in London, where Marilyn was scheduled to begin work on her next picture, *The Prince and the Showgirl*, directed by her costar, Laurence Olivier. Marilyn's working relationship with Olivier was strained. He constantly berated her performance during rehearsals, causing

Marilyn once again to have doubts about her talent. It was as if the positive notices she had received for her work in *Bus Stop* had never happened. Fraught with anxiety, she had trouble sleeping and turned to pills for assistance. The pills often caused her to show up late at the studio. Sometimes, she would not even bother to make an appearance.

After completing *The Prince and the Showgirl*, Marilyn focused her attention on her marriage to Miller. At first, they lived on a farm in Connecticut. Later, they purchased a large apartment in Manhattan. Miller, who believed in Marilyn's dramatic talent, spent his days writing a screenplay for his wife adapted from his short story, *The Misfits*. Marilyn tried unsuccessfully to have a baby.

In 1959 Marilyn starred with Tony Curtis and Jack Lemmon in *Some Like It Hot*. Although the picture is regarded as one of Marilyn's biggest successes, Curtis was particularly dismayed by Marilyn's apparent lack of professionalism. In 1960 Marilyn costarred with French actor Yves Montand in *Let's Make Love*. Dissatisfied with her marriage to Miller, Marilyn reportedly expressed a romantic interest in Montand during the filming.

In 1960 Marilyn began filming *The Misfits* in Reno, Nevada. Clark Gable and Montgomery Clift were signed to costar. Hopes ran high for the movie. Midway through the shooting, it became obvious to everyone involved in the production that Marilyn was too emotionally unstable to be working on a movie. By this time alcohol had joined pills as part of Marilyn's survival strategy. Production was halted for a week, while Marilyn returned to Los Angeles to rest in a hospital. By the time filming was finally completed in November, the picture was millions of dollars over budget, and Marilyn's marriage to Miller was over.

Anxious to resume her acting lessons with the Actors Studio, Marilyn returned to New York. She also admitted herself to a hospital in hopes of treating her depression and dependence on drugs. By the spring of 1962, she was back in Los Angeles, where she was seeing a psychiatrist on a daily basis. Despite this self-imposed break from the pressures of show business, Marilyn still suffered from chronic insomnia. "Nobody's really ever been able to tell me why I sleep so badly, but I know once I begin thinking, it's goodbye sleep," she confided to a reporter. "I used to think exercise helped—being in the country, fresh air, being with a man, sharing—but sometimes I can't sleep whatever I'm doing, unless I take some pills. And then it's only a drugged sleep. It's not the same as really sleeping." To treat her insomnia, Marilyn used an arsenal of prescribed pills, including Librium, Nembutal, and Sulfathallidine.

In 1962 Marilyn began work on *Something's Got to Give*. She was frequently absent from the set, claiming she was suffering from a lingering cold. The gossip columns were filled with stories about Marilyn's friendship with Frank Sinatra. In late May she accepted Sinatra's invitation to fly to New York to sing "Happy Birthday" to President Kennedy at a huge party in Madison Square Garden. While introducing the tardy star, Peter Lawford, the president's brother-in-law, jokingly called her "the late Marilyn Monroe." A few days later she returned to Hollywood and resumed work on *Something's*

Marilyn's performance in *Bus Stop*, the first movie she made after her training at the Actors Studio with Lee Strasberg, is the finest of her career.

The legendary Marilyn Monroe is fixed in our memories in this guise. She is eternally young, effortlessly glamorous, and captivatingly beautiful.

"It's nice, people knowing who you are and all that, and feeling that you've meant something to them."
Marilyn Monroe

Got to Give. On June 1 Marilyn turned 36, and a birthday party for her on the set commemorated the event. A week later, Marilyn was fired from the picture after an unexplained absence of several days. The studio also filed suit against Marilyn, claiming that she had violated her contract.

On August 4, 1962, Marilyn had difficulty sleeping. As usual, she turned to pills. She had also been drinking, and the combination of alcohol and barbiturates proved deadly. The next morning Marilyn's housekeeper, Eunice Murray, was unable to enter Marilyn's locked bedroom. She phoned Marilyn's psychiatrist, who arrived a short while later and discovered her dead body. An autopsy conducted by the Los Angeles County coroner's office ruled that Marilyn Monroe had died from acute barbiturate poisoning. Several years earlier Marilyn had set the stage for her death when she told a reporter, "Yes, there was something special about me, and I knew what it was. I was the kind of girl they found dead in a hall bedroom with an empty bottle of sleeping pills in her hand."

1947-1978

Keith Moon mounts his trusty
steed to ride around the
grounds of his 30-acre estate
near Chertsey in Surrey.

The media chose to focus its attention on Peter Townshend, who wrote many of the Who's songs, and Roger Daltrey, who sang them, but the group's fans understood that drummer Keith Moon was responsible for creating the fun. Onstage and off he was a cutup, and his Moonerisms are legendary. He once nailed a sign to the gateway of his home that read, "Caution— Children at Play." The children were Moon and his friends. Another time he and an accomplice surprised shoppers at a department store, when they walked into a window display featuring a dining room set and ate a meal out of a picnic hamper. "Basically, I'm a frustrated comedian," he once confessed.

Moon enjoyed doing all the crazy things that rock bands on the road are notorious for doing. Partying, wrecking hotel rooms, and throwing television sets out the window were high on Moon's list of fun things to do. The last time the Who played San Francisco, Moon was unable to get the other members of the band to party with him, so he rounded up the stage crew and took over the hotel bar. By the end of the evening, Moonie had smashed everything in the bar that he could get his hands on, including most of the tables and chairs. When it was all over, his assistant laid $2,000 on the bar to cover the damages.

Born on August 23, 1947, Keith Moon was 17 years old when he joined the Who in 1964. At that time the band was known as the High Numbers. A year later, a new management team suggested a different name for the band, which was gaining a reputation for its violent stage antics. The Who were part of the British Invasion that took over American music charts in the mid 1960s. Their first single, "I Can't Explain," was released in early 1965. The song enjoyed moderate success in the United States, but it shot up to the top 10 on British charts. The Who's best known work, their rock opera *Tommy*, was made into a movie in 1975. That year Moon released a solo album, *Two Sides of the Moon*.

Keith Moon died in his sleep on September 7, 1978, from a drug overdose.

The Who were, from left to
right, Roger Daltry, Keith Moon,
Pete Townshend, and John
Entwistle.

Jim Morrison was a legendary figure during his lifetime, and 20 years after his death he remains a legend. While he was the leader of the Doors, Jim worked hard to create his own mythology through his words and actions. Oliver Stone's 1991 movie *The Doors* romanticizes Morrison still further. Jim cut a riveting figure onstage in his skintight leather pants, and when the self-styled Lizard King sang, "No one here gets out alive," he was talking primarily about himself.

James Douglas Morrison was born on December 8, 1943, in Melbourne, Florida. He came from a long line of career military men. Morrison eventually become so estranged from his family that he would claim that both of his parents were dead. Not much is known about Jim's early years, although he claimed that he began writing poetry in sixth grade and continued to fill notebooks with his writings through high school.

Jim fled to Los Angeles in the early 1960s. There he enrolled in film school at UCLA. A classmate described him as "a pudgy kid with hair curling just over his ears, usually dressed in tight wheat jeans and a tight white T-shirt." He read constantly and told his friends that he planned to model his life on that of the hedonistic French poet Rimbaud.

After Jim dropped out of school, he drifted into the hippie scene at Venice Beach, taking LSD freely and sleeping under the boardwalk. One day he ran into an acquaintance from UCLA, Ray Manzarek, who was a keyboardist playing in a struggling rock band. The two shared a six-pack of beer while Jim recited his poem "Moonlight Drive," which later became a song on the Doors' second album. The two decided on the spot to put a group together, even though Jim had no musical experience. Jim later said, "I never did any singing. For the first few songs I wrote I was just taking notes at a fantastic rock concert that was going on inside my head. And once I had written the songs, I had to sing them."

Ray and Jim recruited guitarist Robby Krieger and drummer John Densmore in late 1965 and began calling themselves the Doors. By the following year, the group was paying its dues playing in Sunset Strip dives. Soon, they moved up to more respectable clubs, such as the Troubadour and the Whisky A Go Go. The group quickly became the darlings of the Los Angeles underground. They were known for their hypnotic music and Jim's charismatic stage personality. Although he initially hated the group, Elektra Records president Jac Holzman signed them to a recording contract.

In January 1967 *Doors* was released and received nearly universal acclaim. Many people still consider it the group's best album. Jim was the chief lyricist, and his songs for the album range from the gently flowing "The Crystal Ship" to the explosive "Break On Through" to the Oedipal drama of the 11-minute "The End." "Light My Fire" became the Doors' first hit single, reaching the number-one spot in June.

The group hit the national touring circuit, where Jim's galvanizing stage presence coupled with the rest of the Doors' solid musicianship made

1943-1971

This dramatic image of Jim Morrison in performance was used on the cover of the Doors' album *Live at the Hollywood Bowl*, which was not released until 1987.

The Doors at the height of their fame, from left to right, were Jim Morrison, John Densmore, Robby Kreiger, and Ray Manzarek.

them one of the hottest acts in rock. Their second album, *Strange Days*, was released late in 1967 and features such classics as "People Are Strange," "When the Music's Over," and "Love Me Two Times."

Jim quickly gained a reputation for erratic public behavior. In December 1967 he was arrested onstage at a concert in New Haven, Connecticut, for attempting to incite a riot by telling the audience that police had sprayed him and a friend with mace backstage. The following July the group released *Waiting for the Sun*, which contained the number-one hit "Hello, I Love You." Fueled by drugs and alcohol, Jim's behavior began to get worse. He caused scenes on airplanes, got arrested at airports, and showed up drunk at concerts.

Things came to a head on March 1, 1969, at a concert in Miami, where Jim was arrested for exposing himself to the audience and using public profanity. In Florida these are felony charges and carry a maximum three-year sentence. Because of Jim's legal problems, the group was forced to cancel all their shows for the next five months.

Recorded before the Miami incident, the group's 1969 album *The Soft Parade* kept them on the charts. It features the hit single "Touch Me." The

Jim Morrison, who is better-known for acting out more-sinister fantasies, is assisted by Cathy Christianson in this demonstration of mind over matter.

group followed up in 1970 with *Morrison Hotel* and *Absolutely Live*, neither of which sold well. In August 1970 Jim was acquitted on charges of lewd and lascivious behavior, but found guilty of indecent exposure and profanity. He was sentenced to eight months hard labor but was free upon appeal. He later said, "I really think that it was a life style that was on trial more than any specific incident."

The group made a comeback with their 1971 album *LA Woman*, which was praised in the press and featured the top-20 hits "Riders on the Storm" and "Love Her Madly." Jim decided that he was fed up with being a rock 'n' roll star. In March he and his wife Pamela moved to Paris, where he intended to pursue his literary ambitions. A friend said that "for Jim rock 'n' roll was only a means to an end. He really wanted to be a part of the artistic elite in Europe—a writer or a poet."

On July 3, 1971, Jim Morrison was found dead in his bathtub in Paris. He was 27 years old. The police listed the cause of death as a heart attack. But news of his death was withheld for almost a week, which fueled rumors that he had faked his death. Three years later, Pamela Morrison was dead of a suspected heroin overdose.

Throughout his brief life, Jim Morrison walked a fine line between commercialism and art. His wish to be buried in Père Lachaise cemetery in Paris, where most of France's great literary figures are buried, may show the direction in which he would have liked his life to go.

1947-1979

In the clubhouse locker room, Thurman Munson reads one of his fan letters.

His brief career may have kept Thurman Munson from achieving the stature of New York Yankees legends Babe Ruth, Lou Gehrig, and Joe DiMaggio, but the beloved catcher will always rank as one of the finest players ever to wear the team's pinstripes. Playing his defensive position, he handled pitchers with the care and skill of a psychologist, and five times Munson batted over .300.

Thurman Lee Munson was born on June 7, 1947, outside Akron, Ohio. His father worked as a farmhand. At the age of five, Thurman received his first baseball glove. "After that I started playing baseball every day," he later said. "I was littler than all the rest of the kids, but I played longer every day than any of them." The Munson family later moved to nearby Canton, where in high school Thurman was named all-state in baseball, football, and basketball.

Several major league talent scouts thought Thurman's lack of speed would keep him from ever being a strong prospect to play professionally. But Yankees scout Gene Woodling disagreed. It proved to be one of his more astute observations, and the Yankees selected Thurman as their first choice in the 1968 free agent draft. That same year, Thurman married his childhood sweetheart, Diane Dominick, and dropped out of Kent State University to join the Yankees' farm team in Binghamton, New York, where he batted .301 in 71 games.

Thurman's father was a major influence on the hard-nosed style of Munson's playing. He was also a tough man to please. After his father attended one of Thurman's minor league games, the ballplayer described his dad's reactions: "I think I went five-for-five with a couple of home runs. And after the game he told me I really looked bad behind the plate. To my face he would ridicule me, but to everybody else he would say, 'Hey, that's my son.'"

In 1970, his first full season as a Yankee, Thurman batted .302, and was selected as the American League Rookie of the Year. Like many players, Thurman experienced a "sophomore slump" in his second season, when he batted .251. According to his wife, he spent many of his off-the-field hours "standing in front of the mirror at home, swinging his bat and wondering what he was doing wrong."

Thurman's ability to hit returned, and he batted .280 in 1972 and .301 with 20 home runs in 1973. That same year he won the first of three consecutive Gold Glove Awards for his fielding prowess. Despite this recognition, the unrelentingly competitive catcher was jealous of the attention the press paid to such rivals as Carlton Fisk of the Boston Red Sox. He also began to develop a reputation for surliness with sportswriters.

If he frightened writers, he was popular with his teammates, who made fun of his chunky physique by giving him nicknames like Round Man and Bad Body. Teammate Gene Michael once said, "Everybody likes Thurman

Thurman Munson, Yankee number 15, gets ready to return the ball to the pitcher in a 1970 exhibition game against the Atlanta Braves.

During the 1975 season, the six-time All-Star hit a career high .318, one of five times that he topped the .300 mark in 11 seasons with the Yankees.

and respects him as a ballplayer and a person. Get to know him and he's a friendly, sensitive guy."

In 1975 Thurman had his best season, batting .318 with 102 RBIs—the most by a Yankee in 11 seasons. Before the start of the 1976 season, he was named the first Yankees team captain since Lou Gehrig in 1939. Under their new captain, the team won the American League pennant that year. Thurman hit .302 with 105 RBIs, and won the American League Most Valuable Player Award. He batted .529 against Cincinnati in the World Series, which the Yankees lost.

By the next season, Thurman was beginning to improve his relations with sportswriters. One writer claimed that "he's still no Mr. Congeniality, but he is becoming less the cranky misanthrope that he was." After signing a five-year contract before the 1977 season that made him one of the game's best-paid players, Thurman helped the Yankees defeat the Los Angeles Dodgers for their first world championship in 15 years.

On August 2, 1979, in the middle of the baseball season, Thurman Munson crashed his private plane while trying to land at the Akron-Canton Airport in Ohio. He died on impact.

1940-1985

Ricky Nelson and his older brother, David, joined their mom and dad in the cast of *The Adventures of Ozzie and Harriet* when the show moved from radio to television in 1952.

Child radio and television star, teen idol, and pioneering country-rock singer—Rick Nelson showed many faces to the world. During his teen heart-throb years, Ricky was a tamer version of Elvis, the kind of guy a nice girl could bring home to meet her mom and dad. As he grew up to be a maverick singer-songwriter, his too-good-too-be-true veneer wore away, and even critics who had written him off years earlier began to recognize his talent.

Eric Hilliard Nelson, better known as Ricky, was born on May 8, 1940, in Teaneck, New Jersey, into a popular show-business family. His father, Ozzie, was a bandleader and his mother, Harriet, was the band's singer. Along with his older brother, David, Rick was featured on his mom and dad's radio show. When *The Adventures of Ozzie and Harriet* moved to television, where it ran from 1952 to 1966, the Nelsons became one of America's most famous families.

Jealous of the effect that a young Elvis Presley was having on his girlfriend, Ricky asked his father to help him make a record to impress her. In 1957, after he premiered his version of Fats Domino's "I'm Walkin'" on the family's show, the record sold 60,000 copies in three days and then remained on the charts for five months.

With a guaranteed television audience for his music, Ricky's singles, including "Be-Bop Baby" and "Believe What You Say," were surefire hits. In 1958, when *Life* magazine pictured him on a cover its editors coined a new term to describe him, calling him a teen idol. Fortunately, Ricky was more than just another pretty face. He possessed a softly appealing vocal style. With a top-notch studio band and excellent material, he launched 18 top-10 hits between 1957 and 1964. Among them were such classics as "Poor Little Fool," "Travelin' Man," and "Hello Mary Lou."

When he turned 21 in 1961, Ricky officially became Rick. Recalling his teen idol years, Rick said, "None of that stuff really changed my life much. I was still living at home, and except for a new car, I only got my regular allowance. I didn't even have time for much socializing or parties. I was just too busy with the TV show."

By the time that the Beatles ushered in the British Invasion in 1964, the teen idol phenomenon was on the wane. Luckily for Rick, who had married Kristin Harmon in 1963, the 20-year recording contract that his father had inked for him with Decca Records allowed him to live comfortably for the rest of his life.

Many of Rick's early hits had a country or rockabilly sound, and his work with his Stone Canyon Band in the late 1960s pioneered the country rock style that groups such as the Eagles and Poco would successfully develop. In 1969 Rick scored his first top-40 hit in five years with his version of Bob Dylan's "She Belongs to Me."

An appearance in 1971 at a rock-revival concert in front of an audience of 22,000 at New York's Madison Square Garden helped Rick redefine his career. Because of his long hair and his decision to play his newer material,

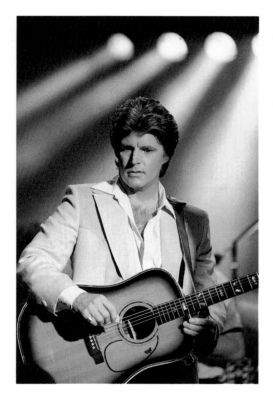

Ricky began singing on television when he was 17 years old. This picture was taken in 1958 at about the time "Poor Little Fool" became a number-one hit.

As a mature country-rock singer, Rick Nelson scored a few hits and toured successfully with his Stone Canyon Band.

Rick was booed by fans who expected to see the old Ricky Nelson. The experience inspired his 1972 hit "Garden Party," in which he sang, "If memories were all I sang, I'd rather drive a truck."

After a five-year separation, Rick and Kristin were divorced in 1982. Kristin won custody of their four children, Tracy, Sam, and twins Matthew and Gunnar. When they turned 18, the twins moved in with Rick at his Hollywood estate. In 1990 as the duo Nelson, Matthew and Gunnar hit the top 10 on their own.

Rick and the Stone Canyon Band tirelessly toured clubs and state fairs, averaging about 200 shows a year. On their way to a 1985 New Year's Eve show in Dallas, their chartered DC-3 caught fire and exploded on landing near De Kalb, Texas. Rick and all the members of the band perished in the crash.

1940-1976

Phil Ochs began his career
singing protest songs and
playing an acoustic guitar.

Phil Ochs was the voice of America's social conscience for almost two decades. Born on December 19, 1940, he grew up listening to Elvis Presley and Buddy Holly, and was a dreamer and loner, who liked to go to the movies two or three times a week. He collected pictures of theater marquees for his scrapbook and knew the winners of every Academy Award that had ever been given. Phil's father decided his son should go to military school and packed him off to Staunton Military Academy, where future Watergate conspirator John Dean was his classmate.

In college, at Ohio State, Phil roomed with Jim Glover, a folk singer, who was a walking manifesto of leftist ideology. He filled Ochs with a sense of empathy for oppressed people, and he lent him his guitar, which Phil took to with ease. Phil wrote articles for the school newspaper denouncing the United States military presence in Vietnam. He tried to publish an essay proclaiming that Fidel Castro was one of the greatest men of the century, but it was refused and he decided to write a song, "The Ballad of the Cuban Invasion." He and Glover performed the number at a local coffee house, and Phil was encouraged to write and sing more songs in his choirboy voice. He figured that because folks liked his music in Columbus, Ohio, they would like it in New York. He dropped out of school and headed for Greenwich Village.

Ochs arrived on the Village scene in 1961. A boom in folk music was underway with the Kingston Trio and Peter, Paul, and Mary singing energized variations of old folk tunes. Ochs and his younger crowd turned their attention to civil rights, banning the bomb, and Vietnam. He was one of the most prolific writers of the group. He came up with a new song every two or three days, and performed them at the Gaslight or the Bitter End, often ending his evenings with Bob Dylan and Tom Paxton, jamming in an Upper West Side apartment.

Phil got his big break at the 1963 Newport Folk Festival. Pete Seeger told him that he was planning to call him onstage to sing a few songs. Ochs was flattered but terrified. He vomited from the rear window of Seeger's car on the way to Rhode Island. By the time he walked onto the stage, Phil had calmed sufficiently to sing "Talking Birmingham Jam," which received a standing ovation. The following year he was invited back as a featured singer.

The times were changing, and songwriters whose lyrics protested traditional values became adored, highly paid culture heroes. Ochs developed a melodramatic flair about his fate now that he had become successful. He was certain that he would be assassinated onstage. At one concert another singer dropped his guitar with a bang. Phil fell to the floor, holding his chest, certain that he had been shot.

In 1967 Ochs released *Pleasures of the Harbor,* his most successful album, with complex musical arrangements that highlighted his maturing talent. Ochs was despondent that the album was not a big hit. The ups and downs

Phil adds his voice and music to one of the large street protests against the Vietnam War.

of his career began to wear on him. His marriage failed, and his wife and daughter moved to California. Ochs claimed he couldn't write anymore, but he experimented with country-Western songs laced with revolutionary philosophy about the significance of Elvis Presley to the workers of the world. His friends tried to bring him through this bad period with therapy and yoga, but nothing seemed to lift his mood. He drank a lot and plotted schemes that never got off the ground.

In 1975, as Christmas approached, Phil asked his sister, Sonny, if he could visit with her and her three children for a few days. He stayed with them in Far Rockaway, New York, for three months, cleaned up his act, and spent time with the kids, who loved to listen to him sing. On the morning of April 9, 1976, his 14-year-old nephew noticed that a kitchen chair was missing from the table and that the door to the bathroom had been shut tight. When he opened it, he found that Phil Ochs had hanged himself.

1950-1988

Christina Onassis lived the kind of life most people can only dream of living. But her all wealth, power, and good looks were unable to give her fairy-tale life a happy ending.

Christina Onassis and Alexandros Andreadis were briefly and unhappily married.

Christina Onassis was born to a life of remarkable luxury. As a child she spent summers on the Greek island of Skorpios, a majestic hideaway, where more than 100 servants cared for life's every detail. In the winter she traveled to the family's lavish chalet in Switzerland. Autumns meant visits to a penthouse in Paris. In spring Christina and her brother shuttled between hotels in London and New York.

During Christina's childhood her father, Aristotle, created a shipping empire that became the world's largest. As she traveled between yachts and homes, anything Christina wanted was immediately available—anything except her parents' attention. Christina was nine when her parents divorced. She became isolated and lonely.

Being a teenager seemed to make everything worse for Christina. She gained weight rapidly and then dieted radically trying to become thin. Her shining eyes and dark Mediterranean features were striking, but she never seemed able to attract a boyfriend. Christina knew that she was less graceful than her mother and could never rival her brother for their father's admiration. As she emerged from school into full adulthood, she struggled to find a place in her family and the world. The cards seemed to be stacked against her. In 1973, when she was 22, her brother was killed in an airplane crash. Two years later, her father died. She attended his funeral with her stepmother, Jacqueline Kennedy Onassis, with whom she barely spoke.

After her father's death, Christina became the first woman to be admitted into the Union of Greek Shipowners. What she most wanted—a happy marriage—remained elusive. Then after three failed marriages in a dozen years, she met Thierry Roussell, the heir to a French pharmaceutical fortune. She was confident that he would bring her happiness. They married and had a daughter, Athina, but Christina discovered that Roussell had a lover and children out of wedlock, and she divorced again.

In 1988 Christina fell in love with an Argentinean businessman, Jorge Tchomlekdjoglou. At last she was ecstatically happy, believing that she had found the right man. On the morning of November 19, while visiting Jorge in Buenos Aires, she was found dead in her bathtub. She had had a heart attack. After three suicide attempts and four marriages, Christina Onassis, one of the world's richest women, died at the age of 37.

■ CHARLIE PARKER ■

Popularly known as Bird, Charlie Parker made music that still mesmerizes jazz fans decades after his death. His innovative flights of fancy on his alto saxophone sound as fresh and daring today as they did in the 1940s and 1950s. Jazz musicians still marvel at his ability to mix amazing speed and dexterity on his instrument with a depth of emotion that even people who do not know jazz cannot help but feel.

Charlie was born on August 29, 1920, in a suburb of Kansas City, Missouri, to Charles Parker and his 18-year-old wife, Addie. When Charlie was seven years old, the family moved to Kansas City proper. At about this time, his father, who had begun working as a Pullman railroad car chef, essentially deserted his family. While he was growing up, music interested Charlie more than school, and when he was 11, his mother bought him an alto saxophone. After spending two consecutive years as a high school freshman, Charlie dropped out to become a musician.

By the time he was 16 years old, Charlie was married and working as a musician in the flourishing Kansas City jazz scene. KC was a wide-open town back then, with gambling and other illicit activities openly taking place in nightclubs while officials turned a blind eye. Living in this kind of environment, Charlie soon began drinking heavily and using drugs. Music was still his main love, and Charlie became a regular at jam sessions, learning from more experienced jazz musicians. He had a lot to learn. At one famous session, drummer Jo Jones became so dissatisfied with Charlie's performance that the drummer stopped playing long enough to throw one of his cymbals at Charlie's feet, "gonging" him off the bandstand in shame.

By the time he was 18 years old, Charlie was living in New York, where he washed dishes at a Harlem restaurant and scrounged music gigs wherever he could. In late 1939 he reached a major breakthrough in his playing that was to revolutionize the jazz world. Tired of playing the same scales when he was playing a solo, Charlie discovered that if he used a higher interval of the chords to a popular song as a melody line, with a pianist or guitarist adding the appropriate new chords, he finally could play the sound that he had always been hearing in his head. Essentially turning the melody line inside out, Charlie began experimenting with this new style that was later called bebop.

Back in Kansas City, he joined the popular Jay McShann band. Thanks to remote broadcasts of the band, musicians all over the country heard his revolutionary playing—even if they did not know his name. Around this time Parker began to be known as Yardbird or more often Bird. He played with McShann until 1942, when he left for brief stints in the big bands of pianist Earl Hines and singer Billy Eckstine. By 1945 Charlie was back in New York and leading his own small groups. He had remarried but continued to live like a nomad, moving from one hotel or boarding house to another. Still a junkie, he also had a prodigious appetite for food. Once he reportedly devoured 20 hamburgers in a single sitting. He was known for his unpre-

1920-1955

Charlie Parker, the best-known author of bebop, created many of the melodies that have become the standard songs of modern jazz, including "Now's the Time" and "Yardbird Suite."

dictable behavior and occasionally tossed his saxophone out of the window of his hotel room.

Charlie took part in what is considered to be the first bebop recording session in 1945. With Dizzy Gillespie and Miles Davis, he recorded "Now's the Time" and "Koko" for Savoy Records. Not long after that he recorded such classics as "A Night in Tunisia," "Yardbird Suite," and "Moose the Mooche" for another small label, Dial Records. These sides polarized the jazz community. For every bebop fan, there was a critic. Band leader Cab Calloway once likened bebop to "Chinese music."

One night in 1946, Charlie went berserk and set fire to his Los Angeles hotel room. He was first taken to the psychiatric ward of the Los Angeles County Jail then later committed for six months to the Camarillo State Mental Hospital. There he wrote one of his best known tunes, the sardonic "Relaxing at Camarillo."

After his release Charlie toured Europe, where he was received like visiting royalty. In the late 1940s, he began experimenting with large string sections and Afro-Cuban rhythms. After a few years of relative stability, he began a downward slide. Parker was back on heroin, nodding out on bandstands, getting into fights, and pawning his saxophones for drug money. Ironically, he always chastised younger musicians who emulated him by using heroin.

Charlie was selected for the *Metronome* magazine All-Stars in 1948. Joining the group marked the beginning of the most successful phase of Bird's career.

In 1948 Bird signed with Norman Granz on the Mercury label, which released this publicity picture. Parker's records now made more money, but his music was somewhat compromised.

Charlie Parker appeared at Birdland for the last time in 1955 just four days before he died. The club, which was named for him, opened in 1948.

By the early 1950s, Bird's self-abuse finally began to infringe on his musical ability. During this time Charlie was befriended by a wealthy European baroness. She was living in New York and loved jazz music and jazz musicians. In 1955, on his way to a gig in Boston, he stopped off at her apartment. Concerned by his apparent ill health, which he blamed on stomach ulcers, she had her doctor examine him. The doctor recommended immediate hospitalization, but Charlie would not even consider it. The baroness got him to agree to rest up at her place for a few days. A few nights later, on March 12, she found him slumped over in an easy chair in front of the television. Charlie Parker was dead at the age of 34. The official cause of his death was listed as lobar pneumonia, and the doctor who performed the autopsy estimated that Charlie was at least 50 years old.

Parker's legend grew even larger after his death. Fans scrawled "Bird Lives!" on the walls of jazz clubs from New York to Los Angeles to Paris. Thirty-five years after his death, Bird remains jazz's single most venerated figure.

1932-1963

Sylvia Plath was an outstanding
American writer, whose novel
The Bell Jar became required
reading for emerging feminists
in the early 1970s.

Like many women of her generation, Sylvia Plath tried desperately to squeeze her extraordinary talents into an ordinary life. Unlike most others, she brought her struggle to the public consciousness through the torturous images of her poems and her novel, *The Bell Jar.* Born in Boston on October 27, 1932, to Aurelia and Otto Plath, Sylvia took her first steps and spoke her first words under the watchful eye of her perfectionist father, who died when Sylvia was five.

She was a brilliant student and always worked hard to exceed the requirements of every assignment. Despite her excellent school record, she feared failure. Attending public school in Wellesley, Massachusetts, Sylvia was always at the top of her class. She published articles and poems in *Mademoiselle* and the *Christian Science Monitor* before she was 18 years old. Sylvia was offered a full scholarship to Wellesley College, but she opted for Smith.

At Smith Sylvia continued to excel. She was elected Phi Beta Kappa in her junior year and named the guest managing editor for *Mademoiselle*'s August 1953 issue. Following a rejection by a summer writing program at Harvard, which she felt was essential to her success as a writer, Sylvia attempted suicide.

Hiding in a cubbyhole in her mother's basement, Sylvia swallowed sleeping pills. Two days later, after the police had made several unproductive searches of the neighborhood, her brother heard a groan from the basement and found Sylvia comatose. Her first lucid words were "Oh no, I've failed!" After a month of electroconvulsive therapy at a mental hospital near Boston, Sylvia returned to Smith and became the valedictorian of the class of 1954. Despite her remarkably quick recovery, the emotional scars of her suicide attempt and the shock treatments are apparent in all Plath's writing.

Sylvia's next triumph was to win a Fulbright fellowship to study abroad. She enrolled at Cambridge University in England and immediately met Ted Hughes, a student writer whose talent was almost equal to hers. Throughout college, vivacious and attractive Sylvia had held off a long string of admirers, but the darkly handsome Hughes captured her heart. They were married on June 16, 1956.

Looking back on Sylvia Plath's life, it is easy to point out this juncture as the place where she went wrong by sacrificing her plans to write to bring about her husband's success as a writer. In her journals she seems clear that this was exactly what she wanted to do, and with Sylvia's help Hughes's book of 40 poems won the 1957 New York Poetry Center Competition for the best first book. That year, Sylvia also gave birth to her first child, Frieda. Initially, she loved the role of mother and caretaker, but the pleasures of caring for a home and a child soon wore thin.

One evening in 1960, Ted Hughes had an interview with a woman who was a BBC producer. He returned home late, and Sylvia became so enraged she tore up his works in progress. To keep the marriage together after

this disaster, Hughes agreed to take over the household chores in the morning so Sylvia could write. *The Colossus*, a collection of her poems, was published in 1960 and hailed as the work of a major poet. Sylvia completed *The Bell Jar* in 1961 while pregnant with her second child, Nicholas.

Before Sylvia had recovered from the birth, she discovered that Hughes was having an affair and decided on a separation. The London winter of 1962-1963 was the most severe in 60 years, and stuck at home with two small children, Sylvia sensed that she was about to have a nervous breakdown. Her physician gave her antidepressants, and for weeks she medicated herself into a stupor that at first alarmed her friends and finally her doctor. On February 11, 1963, her doctor phoned to say that he was sending his nurse to check on her progress. Sylvia told him that she was feeling better.

When the nurse arrived, she found Sylvia sprawled on the floor with the gas oven taps fully turned on. The children were locked in an upstairs bedroom. Under their door several towels blocked off the gas, and tape tightly sealed the cracks. The windows in the bedroom were wide open, and bread and milk was on the table. The children were fine, but Sylvia Plath was gone.

The Collected Poems of Sylvia Plath was awarded the Pulitzer Prize for poetry in 1982. The posthumous award indicates a growing and enduring interest in Plath's work.

1935-1977

Elvis Presley first appeared in Las Vegas, where this photograph was taken, in April 1956. The gig was a disaster because the mostly adult audience did not dig Presley's music or his performance style.

Elvis Presley is one of the true folk heroes of the twentieth century. From humble beginnings he achieved the legendary stature of the King of Rock 'n' Roll. Elvis was born into poverty at the height of the Depression on January 8, 1935, in Tupelo, Mississippi. His twin brother, Jesse Garon, died at birth. Perhaps to compensate for her loss, Gladys Presley showered Elvis with attention. Neighbors recall her walking him to school every morning until he was in his teens. His father, Vernon, worked as a laborer and sharecropper, who spent time in prison for forging a check. One of Elvis's earliest memories was sitting in a truck Vernon drove for a wholesale grocer.

Elvis was first introduced to music at the Pentecostal First Assembly of God church. His family was religious and sang as a trio at camp meetings and revivals. The only kind of music Elvis knew when he was little was gospel music. He once told an interviewer that his family "borrowed the style of our psalm singing from the early Negroes. We used to go to these religious singings all the time. The preachers cut up all over the place, jumping on the piano, moving every which way. The audience liked them. I guess I learned from them."

The first person to recognize Elvis's musical talent was the principal of his grammar school. He encouraged a 10-year-old Elvis to perform in a contest at a local fair. Elvis sang a country-and-western ballad called "Old Shep," which was originally recorded by Red Foley. Elvis's rendition of the song about a boy and his dog was so moving to the judges that he placed fifth in the contest.

On his eleventh birthday, Elvis's parents presented him with a guitar. Elvis could soon be seen carrying the guitar around with him everywhere he went. He even took it to school. He later described his early guitar playing as sounding like "someone beating on a bucket lid." When Elvis was not playing his guitar, he could usually be found curled up next to the radio, listening to music programs. *Grand Ole Opry* was his favorite show, but Elvis occasionally tuned to a station that favored black blues performers, such as Big Bill Broonzy and Big Boy Crudup. If his parents overheard their son listening to the blues, they would tell him to turn it off. They insisted that Elvis listen to and imitate such pleasant-sounding white singers as Roy Acuff, Eddy Arnold, and Jimmie Rodgers.

Shortly after Elvis turned 13, Vernon moved the family to Memphis, where he hoped to find a better job. Shy and introverted, Elvis had trouble making friends at his new school. It was not until he entered a talent show, when he was in the eleventh grade, that Elvis was able to establish a rapport with his classmates. "Nobody knew I sang. I wasn't popular at school. I wasn't dating anybody," he recalled. "I came out and did my two songs and heard people kinda rumbling and whispering." The following day Elvis was besieged by fellow students who suddenly wanted to be his closest friend. "It was amazing how popular I was in school after that."

Hillbilly Cat and the Blue Moon Boys toured the South, stirring up their audiences with Elvis's wild performance style and Bill Blacks's crazy antics with his bass.

In 1956, when this photograph was taken, Elvis was as well known for his exaggerated ducktail haircut, outrageous clothes, and leer that expressed uninhibited sexuality as he was for his music.

Immediately following his graduation, Elvis found work as a driver for Crown Electric. People who knew him then believed that his interest in music would subside and that he would eventually ease into a modest life similar to his father's. Elvis had different ideas. That summer, he visited a recording service run by Sam Phillips, the founder of Sun records, where he cut a demo record. For a $4 fee, Elvis recorded two ballads, "My Happiness" and "That's When Your Heartaches Begin." Several months later, he returned and recorded two more ballads. Once again, he was charged $4. While he was at the recording studio, Elvis took it upon himself to meet with Sam Phillips in the hope of landing a contract. Phillips, who was too busy trying to establish the singers that he already had working under his label, gave Elvis a polite brush-off. By April Phillips had a change of heart. Acknowledging the young singer had potential, he contacted Elvis about cutting a demo, free of charge. Elvis recorded yet another ballad, "Without You," which met with little success.

Despite the record's poor showing, Phillips stood by his conviction that Elvis could succeed as a professional singer. All he lacked was polish. In an attempt to hone Elvis's talents, Phillips introduced him to Scotty Moore, a 21-year-old guitar player. Like Elvis, Moore was anxious to land a recording contract with Sun for his rockabilly band, Doug Poindexter's Starlight Wranglers. The trio went through dozens of songs and experimented with various styles, including country, ballad, and blues, in search of a sound that would best capitalize on Elvis's talents. Finally, Phillips suggested a song originally recorded by Arthur "Big Boy" Crudup called "That's

All Right." Marion Keisker, Phillips's secretary, recalled that this was an inspired choice on her boss's part. "Over and over, I remember Sam saying, 'If I could find a white man who had the Negro sound and the Negro feel, I could make a billion dollars.'"

Elvis recorded "That's All Right" on July 5, 1954. The following day he cut a second song, "Blue Moon of Kentucky," for the record's flip side. Phillips made sure that a preview copy of the single was delivered to Dewey Phillips, the host of a popular Memphis radio show. Dewey, who was no relation to Sam Phillips, was so impressed by Elvis's record that he played it 30 times in one evening. Several weeks later the single was released to record stores with a back order of 5,000 copies. It eventually sold 20,000 copies and enjoyed a brief run as Memphis's top-selling country-Western record. The success of "That's All Right" also led to several stage appearances for Elvis as well as a string of follow-up recordings.

Elvis's popularity was still only local. Setting his sights on national exposure, he hired a manager, Bob Neal, in January 1955. Neal secured an audition for Elvis with *Arthur Godfrey's Talent Scouts* in New York City. The young performer was disappointed to find that his audition had not made the cut. Rather than discouraging him, this setback only served to fuel Elvis's desire to succeed. "He talked not in terms of being a moderate success," explained Neal. From the beginning of his music career, Elvis wanted to be a very big star. But for the time being, he held on to his job as a truck driver for Crown Electric.

A year later Elvis's career quickly changed direction when Colonel Tom Parker entered the picture, succeeding Bob Neal as his manager. Parker, who had managed the careers of country singers Eddy Arnold and Hank Snow, decided that Elvis needed to sign with a major label. Through a series of shrewd negotiations, he was able to secure Elvis's release from Sun records and moved him over to RCA. On January 10, 1956, Elvis recorded "Heartbreak Hotel," his first song for RCA. By the spring it was the country's number-one record. "Hound Dog," which was released several weeks later, also skyrocketed to the number-one position. It was followed by a series of songs that also became hits: "Jailhouse Rock," "Love Me Tender," "Loving You," "Don't Be Cruel," and "All Shook Up."

Appearances on network television soon followed. Elvis appeared with Ed Sullivan, Steve Allen, and Milton Berle. In the span of four short months, Colonel Parker made Elvis a star. "When I first met Elvis," the Colonel once commented to a reporter, "he had a million dollars' worth of talent. Now, he has a million dollars."

The creator of the famous gold lamé suit, Nudie Cohen, poses with Elvis, who wore this legendary outfit during his 1957 national tour.

After Elvis returned to civilian life, he and his manager, Colonel Tom Parker, toned down his appearance to make him look like the leading man he was becoming in Hollywood.

Elvis held three press conferences after his discharge from the Army. First in West Germany, then at Fort Dix, New Jersey, and finally in Memphis, he fended off questions about Priscilla, who had been photographed waving good-bye in Wiesbaden.

In April 1956 Elvis flew to Hollywood, where he made a screen test for producer Hal Wallis at Paramount Studios. A veteran producer, Wallis figured that if people paid to hear Elvis on records, they also would want to see him in movies. Impressed by the screen test, Wallis offered Elvis a three-picture contract. A Western, *Love Me Tender,* was Elvis's first movie. It was released on November 16, 1956. The film was so well received that three weeks after it opened, the studio had already earned back its money. The following summer *Loving You,* Elvis's second feature film, was released. It was also a success.

In December 1957 Elvis received a letter that threatened to end his film and music careers. Elvis had been drafted. He was inducted into the Army on March 24, 1958, and he served for two years, spending most of his stint in West Germany. While Elvis was in the Army, Gladys died. Elvis was devastated by his mother's death and wept openly in front of reporters when he returned to Memphis for her funeral.

After he was discharged, Elvis returned to the United States a changed man. His music had shifted from a hard rock style to a softer pop sound. British rock groups, led by the Beatles and Rolling Stones, eventually eclipsed his popularity. The string of movies he released in the 1960s with such titles as *Girls! Girls! Girls!*, *Kissin' Cousins*, and *Viva Las Vegas* were only vehicles to showcase his singing, but they made Elvis the highest-paid actor in Hollywood.

While he was stationed in West Germany, Elvis fell in love with an Air Force captain's daughter. Her name was Priscilla Beaulieu. On May 1, 1967, they married in Las Vegas, Nevada. The following year Priscilla gave birth to a baby girl, Lisa Marie.

In 1968 Colonel Parker negotiated Elvis's first television special with NBC-TV. The show was a series of polished production numbers designed to capture the essence of Elvis's music. The special was the highest-rated program the week it aired in early December, and critics praised Elvis's perfor-

Elvis and Priscilla were married at the Aladdin Hotel in Las Vegas on May 1, 1967. After a breakfast reception, the couple honeymooned in Palm Springs.

mance. The magic that had been eclipsed by too many improbable movies reappeared. The King of Rock 'n' Roll had regained his throne, and Elvis had made his first gold record in three years: "If I Can Dream."

Elvis's career now entered a third phase that was dominated by live performances. His concerts, which were staged in such large settings as the Houston Astrodome and Madison Square Garden, consistently sold out, and he recorded many of his best-loved hit songs, including "Suspicious Minds," "Kentucky Rain," and "Don't Cry Daddy." Unfortunately, the stress of touring threw Elvis's personal life out of whack. In the early 1970s he and Priscilla divorced. Rumors circulated that he was abusing his body with food, drugs, and alcohol. Fans who traveled to Las Vegas to see him perform were shocked to find that Elvis was overweight. During some shows he could barely sing a complete song because he could not remember the lyrics. On August 16, 1977, Elvis Presley was discovered dead in his bathroom. He was 42 years old.

A moment in the documentary film *Elvis on Tour* captures the way Elvis felt about his life. He said, "When I was a boy I was the hero in comic books and movies. I grew up believing in that dream. Now, I've lived it out. That's all a man can ask for."

On December 3, 1968, Elvis appeared in a prime-time special that brought his magic and charisma to a large audience and launched the third phase of his career in which he became known as America's Greatest Entertainer.

Comedian Freddie Prinze seemed to have everything going for him. He was the star of a hit network television series. Beautiful women were drawn to his good looks and natural charm. He was the father of a baby son. But there were plenty of other things Freddie Prinze had going against him: a failed marriage, a $2,000-a-week cocaine habit, and a morbid fascination with guns.

Prinze grew up in Washington Heights, a poor New York City neighborhood. His mother was Puerto Rican and his father was Jewish. When 16-year-old Prinze made his debut at the Improv, a Manhattan nightclub responsible for launching such talented comedians as Richard Pryor, David Brenner, and Robin Williams, he drew on his mixed heritage to make audiences laugh. Improv's owner Budd Friedman recalled that Freddie was an instant success. Television appearances with Johnny Carson and Jack Paar led to Prinze's being cast at age 19 in *Chico and the Man*, costarring Jack Albertson.

Freddie's rise to stardom was so quick that he often had difficulty accepting it. To ease his insecurities, he turned to cocaine. Prinze's apparent inability to sustain a healthy romantic relationship also created problems for him. Many women were eager to date him, but Prinze doubted their sincerity. He was briefly engaged to Kitty Bruce, the daughter of Freddie's idol, comedian Lenny Bruce. A short-lived marriage to Kathy Cochrane in 1976 produced a son, Freddie Jr.

On January 19, 1977, in the early morning hours, a distraught Prinze called several people, including his personal secretary and his psychiatrist. Marvin Snyder, Prinze's business agent, arrived at his apartment shortly after two in the morning, in response to a call he had received earlier in the evening. While Snyder was in the apartment, Prinze placed calls to his wife and parents. After hanging up, he pulled a pistol from beneath a couch cushion and fired into his right temple. The following afternoon, at UCLA medical center, Freddie Prinze was pronounced dead. Close friends, shocked by the news, speculated that Prinze had not intended to kill himself but was merely playing a prank.

Following his death, police investigators found a note in Prinze's apartment that foreshadowed his intentions. It read simply, "I can't go on."

1954-1977

Even though Freddie Prinze was from New York, he seemed to be a natural for the part of Chico, a young Chicano who lived in the barrio of East Los Angeles.

Freddie Prinze stirs up a little breakfast while Jack Albertson looks on in this scene from their successful television series, *Chico and the Man*.

Through her brilliant comedic work on *Saturday Night Live* in the 1970s, Gilda Radner became one of the greatest television comediennes of all time. For her manic inventiveness, she was often compared to Lucille Ball, and her characters, including Roseanne Roseanadanna, Lisa Loopner, Baba Wawa, and Emily Litella remain as vibrant today as they were when Gilda created them.

A self-characterized "Jewish girl from Detroit," Gilda was born on June 28, 1946. Her family was well-to-do and lived in one of the city's top suburbs. Gilda was overweight as a child, and she always felt that this influenced her desire to become a performer. "When I was ten I said to myself, 'You're not going to make it on looks,'" she later recalled.

Gilda was very close to her father, who often took her to see touring Broadway productions at Detroit's Riviera Theatre. He died of cancer when she was 14, but throughout her life, Gilda's dad continued to be important to her. When she reminisced about him, she would paint a wacky picture of life in the Radner household. "He loved to sing and could tap dance. He couldn't carry a tray of food to the table without tripping to make me and my brother laugh," she said. "If he could have lived another life, he would have been in show biz."

During the time Gilda attended an all-girls high school, she entertained thoughts of becoming a teacher and did volunteer work with emotionally disturbed children. But before she enrolled at the University of Michigan, she had become set on a career in theatre. Following a boyfriend to Toronto, Gilda dropped out of college and joined the cast of the Toronto production of the rock musical *Godspell*. Also in the cast were future stars Martin Short, Eugene Levy, and Paul Shaffer. Gilda later said that she was just a scared little kid when she left Michigan, but she felt that she had to get out on her own and do the things she wanted to do. After her stint in *Godspell*, Gilda joined the Toronto company of the Second City comedy-improv troupe. Other cast members were Gilda's future *Saturday Night Live* cohorts Dan Aykroyd and Bill Murray. A young television producer, Lorne Michaels, who would go on to create SNL, was a regular in the show's audience.

Gilda left Toronto for New York in 1973. She got a bit part as a chanting Buddhist in the movie *The Last Detail*. The following year she became a member of the cast of the syndicated *National Lampoon Radio Hour* and performed in *The National Lampoon Show*, an off-Broadway spinoff of the radio show, which also featured Bill Murray and John Belushi.

When Lorne Michaels was casting the Not Ready for Prime Time Players for the new NBC-TV show *Saturday Night Live*, Gilda was the first performer he hired. The show premiered on October 18, 1975, and was an immediate hit for its irreverent and adventurous brand of comedy. Among the other cast members were Gilda's friends Belushi and Aykroyd, as well as Chevy Chase, Laraine Newman, Jane Curtin, and Garrett Morris.

1946-1989

Gilda Radner was one of the funniest women ever to appear on television. Her sense of timing rivals Lucille Ball's and the large cast of her personal characters is as funny and touching as Lily Tomlin's.

From her ditzy school teacher to her punk rocker, Gilda's characters shine with a sense of themselves that gives them a life of their own apart from their creator. (The man on the left with the upside down guitar is Gilda's first husband, G.E. Smith.)

Saturday Night Live made Gilda the sweetheart of thinking America. Her SNL characters were highly inventive, extremely funny, and yet ultimately sweet. Gilda's large cast of characters included an irreverent newscaster, Roseanne Roseanadanna; a hard-of-hearing, cranky high-school teacher, Emily Litella; a high school nerd, Lisa Loopner; and an excitable prepubescent girl, Judy Miller. Another favorite character is Gilda's Baba Wawa, a take-off on Barbara Walters complete with the commentator's well-known lisp.

While Chevy Chase dominated the program's first season and John Belushi the next two, Gilda became SNL's best-loved cast member. All kinds of people found themselves using punch lines originally delivered by Gilda's characters as part of their day-to-day speech. Emily Litella's "never mind" and Roseanne Roseanadanna's world-weary "It's always somethin'!" continue to pepper our conversations. In 1978 Gilda received an Emmy for best supporting actress in recognition of her stellar work on *Saturday Night Live.*

During the late 1970s, Gilda also was involved with other television projects. She was the Jill of Hearts in a 1977 PBS rock musical, "Jack: A Flash Fantasy," and dubbed the title character's voice in a 1979 animated Halloween special, "Witch's Night Out." But the show other than *Saturday Night Live* that brought Gilda the most acclaim was her 1979 one-woman show, *Gilda Radner—Live from New York.* Appearing off Broadway, Gilda sang, danced, and reprised her popular characters from SNL. *New York Post* critic Clive Barnes said of the show: "From the moment Miss Radner bounces out on stage, beams a twenty-three-carat smile at the audience, and starts to sing the inspired and bawdy 'Let's Talk Dirty to the Animals,' this depraved nymph has won us all over." Warner Brothers released an album of the show, and a year later a filmed version was also issued.

Gilda's personal life was much less successful than her professional life. She always seemed to be searching unsuccessfully for the right man. She once joked that being on SNL for five years kept her from worrying about whether or not she would have a date on Saturday night. The show's producer Michaels remembers that "Gilda had two things that were equally important to her: comedy and having a boyfriend. Unfortunately, she rarely seemed able to do both at the same time." In April 1980 Gilda married guitarist G.E. Smith, who performed with the Hall and Oates band. That same year, after five years in the cast, she left SNL to concentrate on other projects.

Gilda's marriage to Smith was not long-lived. While she was working on the 1982 movie *Hanky Panky*, Gilda fell in love with one of the movie's stars, Gene Wilder. He was 11 years her senior. The nice Jewish girl from Detroit and the nice Jewish boy from Milwaukee immediately clicked, and

Emily Litella, who was everyone's high school English teacher, did not hear very well, but what she thought she had heard often made her extremely upset.

During 1987 Gilda Radner and her husband, Gene Wilder, were able to smile for the camera while Gilda's cancer was in remission.

In a blonde wig and tailored clothes, Gilda became television interviewer Baba Wawa, who was always eager to uncover intimate details and embarrassing secrets.

Wilder wrote a part for Gilda in his next movie, *The Lady in Red*. Gilda once joked that almost as soon as she met Wilder she embarked on a three-year campaign "to get Gene to marry me." She married her prince charming in Paris in 1985.

After their wedding Gilda seemed content to become a Hollywood wife. She took up tennis, learned to like basketball, and happily subordinated her career to Gene's. "I've settled down and gotten off the treadmill," she said at the time. "I've learned that there's much more to life and that I don't have to do everything right away."

In 1986 Gilda began to experience fatigue while filming *Haunted Honeymoon* in Europe with Gene. She visited a slew of doctors when she returned home to Los Angeles and was initially diagnosed as having chronic fatigue syndrome. But Gilda knew it was more than that, and with a family history of cancer, she feared the worst. She began to try alternative forms of medicine, but when her stomach began to swell, she returned to traditional medicine. Her terrible fears were realized when a CAT scan showed she had ovarian cancer.

Shattered emotionally yet outwardly upbeat, Gilda began chemotherapy treatments, which made her even more tired. In 1987 she began to write a book about her battle against cancer, *It's Always Something*, which was published in 1989. For a while Gilda's cancer was in remission, and her book seemed to have a happy ending. By the autumn of 1988, the cancer had returned, and by spring she was down to 95 pounds. At the end of the year, Gilda was talking hopefully about doing a cable television series, but the progress of her cancer was relentless. She died on May 20, 1989, in her sleep at Cedars-Sinai Hospital in Los Angeles at the age of 42. America had lost one of its most beloved comediennes.

Otis Redding has the dubious distinction of being the first recording artist to score a number one hit after he was dead. A plane crash ended his career when it had only just begun, but his posthumous release, "(Sittin' on) the Dock of the Bay," shows what might have been. As his buddy and collaborator Steve Cropper said, "He was the king of soul. Had he lived he would have been the king of them all."

Otis was born on September 9, 1941, in Dawson, Georgia. Like many other rhythm-and-blues performers, Otis grew up singing in church. His dad was a Baptist minister. Throughout high school, Redding idolized Little Richard, who was also born in central Georgia. Otis got so good at imitating Little Richard that he sometimes performed at clubs, pretending that he was his idol.

Redding started his professional singing career recording with Johnny Jenkins and the Pinetoppers, a popular Macon band. In 1962 the combo traveled from Macon to Memphis to audition for Stax Records' boss Jim Stewart. After the band laid down several instrumental tracks, Redding took the mike and sang. He did a Little Richard song, but Stewart said there already was one Little Richard and asked him to try a ballad. Redding sang "These Arms of Mine." Stewart was not swept away, but he recorded the song anyway. It did very well in the South and went on to garner some national attention. Stewart quickly signed Redding to a contract and asked Steve Cropper, the force behind Booker T. and the M.G.'s, to show him the ropes.

Redding's career took off quickly. His 1965 hits "Mr. Pitiful" and "I've Been Loving You Too Long" made him a star and kept him off the "chitlin' circuit" of small clubs and run-down bars, where most rhythm-and-blues singers serve their apprenticeships. A concerted effort to get Otis on the pop charts paid off when his recording of the Rolling Stones hit "Satisfaction" made it to the top 40. Otis didn't know the song, and Cropper brought a copy of the single to the recording session for Otis to learn on the spot. Within a couple of hours, Otis had recorded another big hit, but he never liked the song.

If Redding's career was heating up in the United States, it was red hot in Europe. During 1966 and 1967, Otis played packed houses in Amsterdam and London, and toured the continent several times. Redding needed only a little momentum to take him over the top in the United States. That push came in the summer of 1967 at the Monterey International Pop Festival, which was a coming out party for two black musicians from the opposite ends of the musical spectrum: rock master Jimi Hendrix and soul king Otis Redding.

After Monterey Otis took some time off, relaxed in California, and then went home to Macon to write music. He very much wanted to record a smash single, and he succeeded. From the moment it was finished, Otis knew

1941-1967

Otis Redding had a masterly command of soul ballads, but he could also whip up a whirlwind of excitement with stomping upbeat material, such a "Respect," "Shake," and "Love Man."

Onstage, Redding always gave an energetic and emotional performance, dancing, dropping to his knees, running in place, and getting down with his band.

that "Dock of the Bay" was the monster hit he had been waiting for. On December 6, at the Stax studio, Redding and Cropper laid down the tracks. They added the horns the next day. Then Redding said goodbye and left the studio. He was getting ready to hit the road again, but he never returned.

Three days later, on his way to a concert in Madison, Wisconsin, his airplane tumbled from the sky into the icy waters of Lake Monona. Otis, four members of his back-up group, and the pilot were killed. Otis Redding was 26 years old.

George Reeves, who played Superman on television for six years, killed himself according to the police. But many of his close friends believed he was murdered. They felt that Reeves had everything to live for. He was engaged to marry Lenore Lemmon, a New York show girl, and the couple was planning a honeymoon in Europe. After a two-year dry stretch, Reeves's acting career was thriving again. Production had begun on a new season of *Superman* episodes, and Reeves, who had directed several episodes of the series, had formed his own production company and was planning to direct and star in a science-fiction movie. He was also scheduled to leave on a six-week tour of Australia that would have netted him $20,000. The day he died he was supposed to fight in an exhibition match with boxer Archie Moore. (Before pursuing a show-business career, Reeves considered boxing professionally.) Convinced her son was the victim of foul play, Reeves's mother, Helen Leacher Bessolo, hired criminal attorney Jerry Giesler to launch an independent investigation into George's death.

George Bessolo was born on April 6, 1914, in Ashland, Kentucky. When he was seven years old, his family moved to southern California. In high school George expressed an interest in acting and performed with several theater groups. After enrolling in Pasadena Junior College, he participated in a string of boxing matches, much to his mother's dismay. At six feet two inches and 195 pounds, George was a promising light heavyweight. He competed in the Golden Gloves in 1932-1933 but put boxing aside after his nose was broken for the seventh time. From then on, Bessolo focused exclusively on his acting career. While serving an apprenticeship at the Pasadena Playhouse, he caught the eye of casting director Max Arnow, who gave him a featured role as one of the Tarleton twins in *Gone With the Wind*. While Bessolo was working as a contract player at Warner Bros., he was renamed George Reeves. He appeared in several pictures, including *Lydia*, opposite Merle Oberon, and *So Proudly We Hail*, starring Claudette Colbert. His acting career was interrupted by a stint in the Army, where he served as an entertainer during World War II. After his discharge Reeves had difficulty landing any movie roles. In 1951 he was cast to play Superman in a low-budget feature. Production of the television series *The Adventures of Superman* began the same year. The role proved to be a mixed blessing: It gave him financial security, but he became so closely identified with the superhero that casting directors were reluctant to use him for other parts.

On June 16, 1959, at about 1:30 A.M., Reeves was awakened by friends visiting his fiance. Upset by their noisy socializing, Reeves demanded that they leave. He then returned to his upstairs bedroom. "Well, he's sulking now," Lemmon reportedly told her friends. "He'll probably go shoot himself." In the next instant, a gunshot was heard. Reeves's nude body was discovered in the bedroom. On the floor next to him was a .30-caliber Luger. When police arrived a short time later, they had difficulty getting a coherent account

1914-1959

In a dramatic moment, Superman, disguised as Clark Kent, receives a call for help that demands his immediate action.

Superman (George Reeves) and Lois Lane (Phyllis Coates) are worried by the doctor's report in this scene from the 1950s television series.

from Lemmon and her houseguests because everyone had been drinking heavily. Based on their preliminary findings, the police decided that Reeves had killed himself.

Giesler's investigation suggested that Reeves had been murdered. A private detective uncovered evidence that two shots were fired the night Reeves died. "Suicides very rarely have a chance to shoot twice," commented a skeptical Giesler. It was also revealed that several months before Reeves's death, he was the victim of a series of harassing phone calls. He confided to police that he believed the caller was a married woman with whom he had recently broken off. A police investigation determined that she was not making the calls. "Then who the hell is after me?" asked Reeves. The police were never able to provide him with an answer. As mysteriously as the calls began, they suddenly stopped. Despite the strange circumstances surrounding the death of George Reeves, the police refused to reopen their investigation.

In the early 1980s, network newscaster Jessica Savitch was skyrocketing toward the heights of her profession, but she also suffered several personal tragedies: a divorce from her first husband, the suicide of her second, and a miscarriage.

Savitch was born on February 1, 1947. Her father died suddenly when she was 12 years old. Jessica idolized her father and was hit hard by his death. She credited him with introducing her to television news. At mealtimes he encouraged his children to participate in lively discussions about world events. In high school Savitch first considered a career in broadcasting. She had a friend who worked part time as a radio disc jockey, and he helped her get a job spinning records. When Savitch decided to major in communications at Ithaca College in New York, her faculty advisor bluntly told her, "There's no place for broads in broadcasting." Savitch set her sights on proving him wrong.

After her graduation Savitch became a researcher for CBS-Radio. In 1971 she landed a job at KHOU-TV in Houston. Three months later, Savitch enjoyed the distinction of becoming the first woman in the South to anchor a newscast. Unfortunately, Savitch's drive came with a price. "From the beginning, from college on, she never had a personal life," her college roommate observed. In 1972 Savitch accepted an offer to anchor an evening newscast in Philadelphia. Within weeks the program jumped to first place in the ratings, and the networks came calling. In 1977 Savitch signed a contract with NBC to anchor their Sunday evening newscast. When NBC incorporated 60-second news updates into its prime-time programming, Savitch was tapped to anchor them.

Savitch's meteoric rise inspired resentment among her colleagues, who felt she hadn't paid her dues by first working as a network correspondent. Her intense desire for perfection did not help to ease their jealousy. On October 3, 1983, Savitch's antagonists finally found reason to celebrate. During a live update, Savitch appeared incoherent. Her speech was slurred. She deviated from the copy and ad-libbed her report. Later, Savitch explained that her monitor had malfunctioned. Inadvertently contradicting Savitch's alibi, her agent told the media she was on medication, following an accident when a sailboat boom struck her in the face several weeks earlier. Rumors spread through NBC that Savitch was using cocaine.

A short while later, Savitch's life seemed to get back on track. Her contract at NBC had been extended. Besides subbing for Chris Wallace on Sunday's evening newscast, *Today*'s producer, Steve Friedman, ranked her high on the list of replacements for Jane Pauley, who was scheduled to take a maternity leave. She was also promised a visible role in the network's upcoming election coverage. Savitch had begun dating Martin Fischbein, a *New York Post* executive. Her friends felt that he had a calming effect on her.

1947-1983

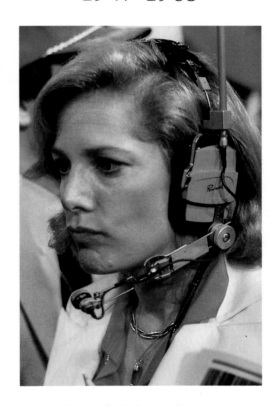

Jessica Savitch at work on a live report: Had she lived, she would have had major responsibilities for NBC's coverage of the 1984 elections.

Posed outside the Capitol, NBC correspondent Jessica Savitch reports on "The Spies Among Us" for a network news program.

On Sunday, October 23, 1983, Savitch did something completely out of character. She scheduled a full day for nothing but relaxation. That morning, she and Fischbein rented a car and drove to New Hope, Pennsylvania, where they leisurely shopped for antiques. At six-thirty they arrived at Chez Odette, a restaurant alongside the Delaware Canal. Their hopes for a long, romantic dinner were dashed by a sudden change in weather. A fierce rainstorm had set in. Anxious to return to New York, the couple completed their meal in 45 minutes. Fischbein drove, and Savitch settled in the backseat with Chewy, her Siberian husky. Weather conditions made driving difficult. Soon after leaving the restaurant, Fischbein apparently mistook a dirt road for an exit. In a matter of seconds, the car flipped and plunged into the canal. Approximately seven hours later, the bodies of Jessica Savitch and Martin Fischbein were pulled from the canal.

Del Shannon was a uniquely self-contained talent. He wrote, performed, and often produced his own material in a classic pop-rock style that was absolutely his own. His arrangements are an astounding combination of high-pitched keyboard music, rapid-fire rhythm, and Shannon's own assailing falsetto.

He was born on December 30, 1939, in Cooperville, Michigan, and named Charles Westover. As a teenager, he took the name Shannon from a local pro wrestler. The name Del comes from Cadillac Coupe de Ville. Unable to play a ukulele that he was given on his 13th birthday, Del traded it in for a used guitar. He taught himself to play and improved his style by watching guitarists at country-Western dance halls. Del Shannon really did learn to sing in the shower. His football coach even encouraged his in-the-shower shows and eventually convinced him to entertain at school assemblies.

After serving with an Army entertainment unit, Shannon returned to Michigan and took a part-time job selling carpet. He also organized his first band. Disc jockey Ollie McLaughlin was so impressed by Shannon's voice that he convinced a Detroit record company to take him on. His first recording session was a total bust. Shannon stumbled through a few ballads and the record company producers told him to go back to peddling carpets—which he did.

Still undeterred, McLaughlin instructed Shannon to concentrate on up-tempo material, and Del began to develop the quick chord changes that were to become his signature. After he wrote "Runaway," McLaughlin took the song to another record company, Big Top Records. In 1961, only three months after it was released, "Runaway" was a monster single, topping the charts for 12 weeks. Later that year, Del followed up his successful first record with a pair of hits, "Hats Off to Larry" and "So Long Baby."

On Shannon's first European tour in 1963, he encountered Beatlemania for the first time. Knowing a trend when he saw one, Del immediately recorded John Lennon and Paul McCartney's "From Me to You." Shannon's record was the first Beatles tune to hit the American charts.

By the mid 1960s, Del's records were no longer selling very well in the United States. But he was a popular star in Europe, especially in England, and his overseas record sales remained strong. In 1962 and 1963, Shannon was named the Most Popular Male Vocalist in England.

When his career had started to flag, Shannon hurt his cause by repeatedly suing Big Top Records and his own manager. In 1963 he attempted to launch his own label, but the company was a dud. Other labels were reluctant to take on a litigious artist, and in 1964 only Amy Records was willing to sign Shannon. That year he made the charts with his version of the Jimmy Jones's hits "Handy Man" and his own "Keep Searchin'."

1939-1990

In 1961 Del Shannon recorded "Runaway" with keyboardist Max Crook. The single stayed at the top of the chart for 17 weeks.

The 1980s saw Del rebound with *Drop Down and Get Me*. Rock critics loved the album, and fans were eager to see Del in concert.

Although Shannon would later consider a guitar essential to his performance, during the early part of his career he was often featured as a vocalist.

Shannon's refusal to take direction from his recording company eventually led to a break with Amy Records. Without a label Shannon found work producing for other musicians. In 1970 he produced Brian Hyland's "Gypsy Woman." British rocker Dave Edmunds attempted to rebuild Shannon's recording career in 1974, but he was not successful. Tom Petty had better luck as Del's producer in 1981, when he released the album *Drop Down and Get Me*. The single release "Sea of Love" put Shannon back on the United States pop charts for the first time in 15 years. When there were no further record deals and no concert bookings, Shannon realized that a comeback was not in the offing.

On February 8, 1990, Shannon's wife LeAnne returned to the couple's Santa Clarita, California, home and found her husband laying on the floor in their den. He had been fatally wounded by a gunshot. A .22-caliber rifle was lying next to Shannon's body. The official cause of his death was listed as suicide. Del Shannon was 50 years old.

From his earliest childhood, Ritchie Valens associated music with happy times. Whenever his family gathered, they played music. At the age of six, Ritchie learned to strum a guitar, sitting on the knee of a family friend. Although Ritchie only spoke English, his uncle taught him to sing "La Bamba," a Spanish folk song, in Spanish. Years later, teenagers all over America would dance to Ritchie's rock 'n' roll version of "La Bamba."

Ritchie Valens, who was born on May 13, 1941, grew up in the San Fernando Valley. When he was 11 years old, his father died suddenly. His widowed mother, Connie Valenzuela, struggled to provide for her young son and his two younger sisters. To help her pay the bills, Bob Morales, Connie's son from an earlier marriage, moved in with the family. Unfortunately, Bob had a drinking problem. Although Connie appreciated the additional money he brought in from his job as a garbage collector, she found his drinking difficult to accept and quarreled frequently with him. The tension Bob's presence created in their household made Ritchie uneasy. To escape from the fighting, he turned to his music.

When he was 17 years old, Ritchie met Bob Keene, a local record promoter. Keene agreed to listen to some of Richie's original songs. "That's My Little Suzie," which he based on a crippled girl he knew from his barrio, particularly impressed Keene. He also liked Ritchie's rock 'n' roll version of "La Bamba" and decided to manage his career. Within six months Los Angeles disc jockeys were spinning Ritchie's tunes. His first hit, "Come on, Let's Go," was released in September 1958. Ritchie got the title from an expression he and his mother used whenever they wanted to go somewhere. In fact, Connie had just used the expression minutes before she heard Ritchie's music on the radio for the first time. "I told his brother Bob, 'Come on, let's go to Saugus (a nearby community).'" While they were driving, "Come on, Let's Go" came over the radio in Connie's 1950 Oldsmobile. She pulled over to the side of the road and just sat there looking at Bob amazed.

Donna Ludwig, Ritchie's high school girlfriend, was the inspiration for his biggest hit, "Donna," which was released in November 1958. Shortly after writing the tune, Ritchie called Donna and said, "I wrote a song for you." The first time Donna heard the song was when Ritchie played it for her over the phone. He also promised to record it, but Donna doubted he would because she thought he only released "upbeat stuff." But a short time later, when Donna and some of her girlfriends were riding down the main drag in San Fernando in her convertible, they heard the song on the radio. She recognized "Donna" from the time Ritchie played it for her over the phone. Her girlfriends started screaming, and like Ritchie's mother, Donna pulled her convertible over to the side of the road. She and the girls sat in the car and cried because the song was so pretty.

1941-1959

Ritchie Valens had a big impact on rock music even though his death at age 17 cut short his promising career as a singer and composer.

Bob Keene, president of Del-Fi Records, discovered Ritchie while he was singing at a dance with his group, the Silhouettes.

To promote his single "Donna," with "La Bamba" as its flip side, Ritchie went on a nationwide tour as part of a rock 'n' roll show that also featured Buddy Holly and the Big Bopper. On February 3, 1959, en route to Fargo, North Dakota, their plane crashed in a cornfield in Clear Lake, Iowa. "It took them eight days to send Ritchie's body back from Iowa," his mother recalled. "They didn't send him to me by plane. Instead, they sent him on a train to San Fernando." The same morning Ritchie's body arrived at the mortuary, Keene showed up with a copy of Ritchie's first album. "It had been released in those eight days since his death," explained Connie. "I originally wasn't going to play the album because it was too painful. But I finally put on a brave front and said to myself, 'I'm going to play this before I bury him,' and I did."

Stevie Ray Vaughan was a unique musician who mixed Texas blues with guitar riffs inspired by Jimi Hendrix. While he was growing up, his parents often held dance parties at their house near Dallas. Bob Wills's band, the Texas Playboys, were frequent visitors. Sometimes the musicians would hold an impromptu jam session, mixing contemporary hillbilly, swing, and country tunes. Stevie's older brother Jimmie belonged to a band, and an enthusiastic Stevie sat in on their practice sessions. When it came to buying records, the brothers also shared similar tastes, preferring blues albums recorded by B.B. King, Buddy Guy, and Albert Collins.

Born on October 3, 1954, Stevie was 14 the first time he performed professionally. He was a member of several bands including Blackbird, the Chantones, the Epileptic Marshmallow, and Cracker Jack. For a brief period, he was also the bass player in Jimmie's band, Texas Storm. In 1973 Stevie started his own band, the Nightcrawlers, but he soon left it to join a rhythm-and-blues combo, the Cobras. In 1977 he joined Triple Threat, a band that boasted three lead singers, including Lou Ann Barton. In the late 1970s Vaughan and Barton formed a new band, Double Trouble, and by 1981 the band consisted of Vaughan, bassist Tommy Shannon, and drummer Chris "Whipper" Layton.

Record producer Jerry Wexler heard Vaughan performing in an Austin club and arranged for the band to perform at the 1982 Montreux Jazz Festival. Double Trouble was the first band to perform at the festival without a record. David Bowie was in the audience and later approached Vaughan about playing on his next album, *Let's Dance*. He played guitar on six of the album's tunes, exposing his talents to a completely new audience.

Vaughan's debut album, *Texas Flood*, was released in June 1983. In 1985 Vaughan received his first Grammy for his track on *Blues Explosion*. A year later, while performing in London, Vaughan collapsed on stage. He checked into a clinic to receive treatment for his drug and alcohol problem. Following his release from the clinic, a recovered Vaughan resumed performing. In 1990 Vaughan received his second Grammy for *In Step*.

On August 27, 1990, Vaughan performed with Eric Clapton at an outdoor concert in Wisconsin. Following the concert, Stevie Ray Vaughan boarded a helicopter to fly to Chicago. Clapton boarded a second helicopter. Shortly after taking off in a dense fog, Vaughan's helicopter crashed into a hill. There were no survivors.

1954-1990

Two-time Grammy winner, Texas blues man Stevie Ray Vaughan was on the brink of superstardom when his helicopter crashed into a Wisconsin hillside.

1904-1943

In the 1942 movie *Stormy Weather*, Fats Waller stole the show simply by the way he raised his eyebrows while he played the piano.

Fats Waller, who was born on May 21, 1904, began his musical career at the age of eight when he played reed organ for his father, Edward Waller, a Baptist lay preacher in Harlem. Fats also entertained his classmates banging on the piano in school. The elder Waller encouraged his son to practice his God-given gifts exclusively in the church. This became a constant source of friction in the Waller house. At age 15 Fats accepted a job as an organist at the Lincoln Theatre on 135th Street.

Unable to live with his disciplinarian father any longer, 16-year-old Fats moved in with pianist Russell Brooks and his family. He studied classical music with Leopold Godowsky and also enrolled in composition classes with Carl Bohm at the Juilliard School. Musician James P. Johnson helped the young man develop his skills as a pianist and got him work making piano rolls. In 1922, with Johnson's assistance, Fats sold his first song, "Got to Cool My Doggies Now." Encouraged by this success, Fats married Edith Hatchett, his childhood sweetheart. Soon, Edith gave birth to a baby boy.

That year, Fats made his recording debut as a soloist. His recordings became so popular that several blues singers, including Sara Martin, Alberta Hunter, and Maude Mills, hired Fats to accompany them as pianist on their own recordings. A year later, Fats established his reputation as a composer when he collaborated with Clarence Williams on "Wild Cat Blues." That same year, Fats also made his broadcasting debut for a Newark radio station and began making regular appearances on New York's WHN. By 1929 Fats had recorded several of his own creations, including "Honeysuckle Rose" and "Black and Blue." He also teamed with producer Andy Razaf to score music for the all-black musical *Keep Shufflin'*, which premiered on Broadway in 1928. They wrote two more shows in 1929, *Load of Coal* and *Hot Chocolates* with the show stopper "Ain't Misbehavin'."

Close friends of the gifted musician who witnessed firsthand his extravagant food binges understood how he earned the nickname Fats. He also drank too much. After Fats and Edith divorced, his failure to pay alimony regularly added legal problems to Fats's other worries. In 1926 Fats fell in love with a 16-year-old named Anita Rutherford. After a brief courtship, they married. A year later, Anita made Fats the father of a second son.

In 1929 Fats drew a prison term for failing to make alimony payments to his ex-wife Edith. While he was behind bars, his father died. When Fats was released from jail, Anita informed him she was pregnant again. Later that year, she gave birth to another son.

In 1935 Fats appeared in two Hollywood movies, *Hooray for Love!* and *King of Burlesque*. He also made his most successful record, "I'm Gonna Sit Right Down and Write Myself a Letter." His arrangement was so popular that people believed he had written the song.

By the early 1940s, Fats's drinking was ruining his health. He would down a case of scotch during a rehearsal with his band. His drinking was also

destroying his career. He skipped concert dates, claiming he had a bad cold, and he made poor choices of material. Jazz critics and fans alike felt he squandered his talent recording inferior songs.

In early 1943 Fats traveled by train from New York City to Los Angeles for a series of concert dates. On the trip back to New York, Fats suddenly took ill. As the train approached Kansas City, in the early morning hours of December 15, 1943, Fats Waller was discovered dead in his berth. While his train was delayed in Kansas, another train sat next to it on the tracks waiting for clearance to continue its journey. On board was Louis Armstrong who was overcome with emotion by the news of his friend and colleague's sudden death.

After recording "I'm Gonna Sit Right Down and Write Myself a Letter" in 1935, Waller became better known as a singer than he was as a jazz pianist.

1923-1953

Hank Williams wrote most of the songs that everyone associates with country music: "Move It On Over," "I Saw the Light," "Six More Miles," "Your Cheatin' Heart," and many more.

Hank Williams continues to be one of the major country music stars. His classic songs, including "Your Cheatin' Heart," "Hey, Good Lookin'," and "Jambalaya," remain country standards. His musical style and his dynamic personality have endured the test of time and left their mark on today's country stars, such as Randy Travis, Dwight Yoakam, and George Strait.

Hank's special genius captures an emotion in the lyrics of his songs and expresses it in a voice that was tailor-made for his often dark and troubled music. His vocal style is the essence of what used to be called hillbilly music. Hank's enduring songs and tragically dissipated personal life continue to fascinate new generations of fans.

Hank was born on September 17, 1923, in a small Alabama farming community about 70 miles south of the state capital of Montgomery. His father was a railroad engineer, who was a victim of shell shock in World War I and spent many years in veterans' hospitals. Hank's mother, who played the organ in church, began to teach her son gospel songs when he was just a little boy. By the time he was six, Hank was one of the youngest members of the church choir.

His parents bought him a guitar for his eighth birthday, and he taught himself to play by watching other guitarists, including a black street musician known as Tee-Tot. In his early teens, Hank was teaching himself to play and sing the country songs that he heard on the family's radio. He also started to sit in with other musicians. When he was 14 years old, Hank put together his own band, playing at hoedowns and other get-togethers. He also began to see such country stars as Roy Acuff whenever they passed through the southern part of Alabama for a live appearance.

Hank called his group the Drifting Cowboys, and they successfully auditioned for the manager of WSFA in Montgomery. He hired Hank and the band to perform regularly on the air. This association lasted for the next 10 years. Although Hank and the Drifting Cowboys were becoming well known regionally, it was only after he married his first wife, Audrey, that his reputation began to spread beyond his native Alabama. Hank and Audrey met at a traveling medicine show. In 1944 they were married at an Alabama gas station. Audrey was a strong-willed woman who was happy to take control of Hank's career. She became his booking agent, road manager, and best promoter, and the shy singer was more than happy to relinquish these responsibilities to his wife. Audrey immediately began to increase the number of gigs Hank and his band played and to book shows outside Alabama.

Hank Williams and his band, the Drifting Cowboys, played together for more than 10 years. The fiddler behind Hank is Jerry Rivers.

By 1946, when he and Audrey traveled to Nashville to secure a music publishing contract with the influential producer Fred Rose, Hank was already writing some of the songs that were to make him a country music superstar. Rose, who was the head of the Acuff-Rose publishing firm, listened to a nervous Hank Williams sing several of his original songs. As a test, Rose asked Hank to write a song on the spot. The result was "Mansion on the Hill," a song that not only got Hank a publishing contract with Acuff-Rose but later became an often-recorded country standard. Over the next few years, Hank became the firm's most successful songwriter.

In 1947 the skinny singer in his signature white cowboy hat had a banner year. MGM Records signed Hank to a recording contract, and he also became a regular on the *Louisiana Hayride* radio show on KWKH in Shreveport, Louisana. This country music program was second in prestige only to the *Grand Ole Opry* on Nashville's WSM. Their appearances on the *Hayride* helped Hank and his band achieve their first hit, "Move It On Over." In 1949 Audrey gave birth to Hank Jr. Adding to the successes of that year, Hank also was asked to join the Grand Ole Opry. He made his debut on the Opry stage at Ryman Auditorium on June 11, 1949. Giving Hank a taste of what was to come, the audience demanded an unprecedented six encores.

Hank soon became country music's top artist. Among his hits in 1949 and 1950 were "Lovesick Blues," "My Bucket's Got a Hole in It," "Moanin' the Blues," and "Why Don't You Love Me." In 1951 Hank kept his string of hits going with "Hey, Good Lookin'," "Cold, Cold Heart," and "I Can't Help It." One of the first signs that Hank was more than just another hillbilly singer was Tony Bennett's successful pop rendition of "Cold, Cold Heart."

Hank's unprecedented success rate continued in 1952 as he cemented his position as country music's number-one artist. Among those hits were "Honky Tonk Blues," "Jambalaya," and the prophetic "I'll Never Get Out of This World Alive." While he was scoring one smash hit after another, Hank's self-destructive tendencies were beginning to have an effect on his career. A heavy drinker since his teen years, Hank began to mix booze with pills. This combination began to give him a reputation as an undependable performer who often showed up drunk and drugged—if he showed up at all. One of his proteges told the *Rocky Mountain Musical Express*, "Up to a point, liquor and pills just made him sing better and better. Then, all of the sudden, he'd just cave in. Sometimes he'd get real mean. You never knew which way he was going to go."

Hank and Audrey began to fight on an almost daily basis, and Audrey divorced him in 1952. Williams's well-known song "Your Cheatin' Heart" was reportedly inspired by Audrey. His relationship with both close friends and his band began to sour as well. In a humiliating move, the Grand Ole Opry suspended him from appearing on the show.

In 1952 Hank married 19-year-old Billie Jean Jones, who was no more successful than Audrey had been in protecting Hank Williams from himself. Unable to put up with his violent mood swings and unpredictability, the

The signature Hank Williams look was a well-cut Western suit tailored by Nudie Cohen, a hand-painted tie, hand-tooled boots, and a top-of-the-line five-gallon Stetson hat.

Drifting Cowboys parted ways with Hank that year. Williams died in his sleep in the backseat of his Cadillac on January 1, 1953, while traveling through West Virginia on the way to a show in Canton, Ohio. Hank Williams was 29 years old.

After his death many of the people who had given up on Hank during the last years of his life began to lionize him. His funeral in Montgomery attracted 25,000 people, and he continued to have hits after his death as MGM Records began to repackage his music, often adding strings and backup singers to his rather spartan arrangements. Many critics felt that Hank Williams had not been aware of the true magnitude of his talent. He lived liked a nomad, traveling through the South with his band and then blowing into Nashville and staying just long enough to make a new record before hitting the road again. Like other country musicians in the 1940s and 1950s, Hank Williams was under constant physical and emotional stress trying to make a living from his music.

Even as the country music world watches Williams's son Hank Jr. become a country music star in his own right, often singing about the father he barely knew, everyone knows there is only one Hank Williams. Elected to the newly established Country Music Hall of Fame in 1961, his plaque is a fitting epitaph. It reads in part, "Performing artist, songwriter Hank Williams will live on in the memories of millions of Americans. The simple, beautiful melodies and straightforward, plaintive stories in his lyrics of life as he knew it will never die. His songs appealed not only to the country music field, but brought him great acclaim in the pop music world as well."

The signature Hank Williams look was a well-cut Western suits tailored by Nudie Cohen, hand-painted ties, hand-tooled boots, and a top-of-the-line five-gallon Stetson.

1944-1983

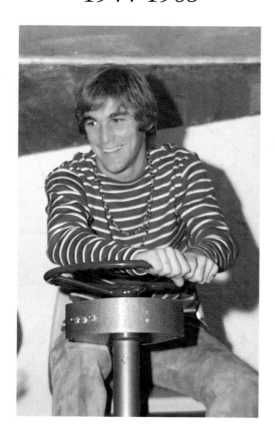

Dennis was the only Beach Boy
who was a surfer; it was a style
of life he never gave up.

Of the five original members of the Beach Boys, Dennis Wilson was the only one who knew how to surf. His brother Brian was afraid of the water. Dennis grew up in Hawthorne, California, a working-class suburb of Los Angeles. His father owned a machine shop and was a frustrated songwriter. His mother enjoyed singing and frequently organized family sing-alongs. Brian, the oldest son, was humming complete songs when he was just 11 months old. At three he was singing them. By sixteen, with the use of a small tape recorder, Brian created four-part harmonies. Carl, the youngest brother, taught himself to play the guitar when he was 11 years old. Cousin Mike Love was known for having perfect pitch. Dennis, who was born on December 4, 1944, was a maverick. He had no interest in music until he was in his teens, when he learned to play the drums.

In 1961 Brian came up with the idea for the band that would become the Beach Boys, but Dennis inspired their first hit. The original band had five members: the three Wilson brothers, Mike Love, and Al Jardine, who was in college with Brian. They wanted a recording contract with a major label and knew they would have to create a fresh sound. The band spent many afternoons brainstorming until Dennis came up the right idea. He thought they should record a song about surfing. By the next afternoon, Brian had written "Surfin'," which became a hit in Los Angeles and helped the Beach Boys secure a recording contract with Capitol records.

By 1966 Brian had become bored writing songs that celebrated sun worshiping. The Beach Boys released *Pet Sounds* in 1966. The theme album explores the emotions that people experience as they move toward maturity. In 1970 Dennis released a solo single: "Sound of Free" and "Lady," which he recorded with Daryl Dragon, who had been an auxiliary keyboardist for the Beach Boys. The following year, Dennis costarred in the movie *Two-Lane Blacktop*, which proved to be a box-office disaster.

For Dennis the late 1960s was a time of upheaval in his personal life. He divorced his wife Carol and soon found himself caught up in a lifestyle where drugs were readily available. He even hung out with convicted murderer Charles Manson. Together they wrote a song, "Never Learn Not to Love." It was included on the Beach Boys album *20/20*, released in early 1969. Dennis's friendship with Manson ended abruptly when Manson became incensed that he was not given a published credit for writing the song. Following the Tate/LaBianca murders, Dennis received threatening calls from Manson's cult warning him that he was next. He often awoke in the morning to find that the furniture in his home had been mysteriously rearranged during the night. Dennis relaxed after Manson was securely behind bars.

In the 1970s Dennis married his second wife, actress Karen Lamm. A short while later, they divorced, then remarried, and finally divorced again. He also fathered a child by the daughter of his cousin Mike Love. Dennis's battle to overcome a long-standing drinking problem influenced his decision

On the Beach Boys' first single, "Surfin'," Dennis beat rhythm on a garbage can, but success brought him a more conventional drum set.

Ready to set out on a surfin' safari, Dennis Wilson loads a surfboard into the Beach Boys' old yellow truck. This picture became the album cover for the group's first LP.

to stop touring with the Beach Boys in the early 1980s. His disappointment over the band becoming nothing more than a group of middle-aged men lifelessly playing oldies also played a role in his getting out.

On December 28, 1983, Dennis Wilson spent the day doing something he had enjoyed his entire life: swimming in the Pacific Ocean. Despite the water temperature being a cool 58 degrees, Wilson chose not to wear a wetsuit. For two straight hours, he entertained himself diving 13 feet into the water. Then suddenly, he lost his balance and slipped. When friends noticed he had not surfaced, they became alarmed and phoned the police. An hour later, Wilson's body was discovered. An autopsy ruled the cause of his death to be accidental drowning—an ironic way for a Beach Boy's life to end.

1938-1981

As a mature actress, Natalie Wood was especially good in a comic role as Mari in the 1980 movie *The Last Married Couple in America.*

One of Hollywood's most beautiful actresses, Natalie Wood was also one of the few performers who successfully made the transition from child star to adult star. Her incredible natural beauty often prevented critics from taking her seriously as an actress, but her three Oscar nominations speak for her talent.

She was born Natasha Gurdin on July 20, 1938, in San Francisco to a Russian father and a French mother. As a child Natalie spoke several languages and studied dance. (Her mother, Maria, had been a ballerina.) Natalie made her screen debut at age four in the 1943 movie *Happy Land*, which director Irving Pichel was filming in the family's hometown of Rosita, California. Several years later he cast her to play a German refugee in *Tomorrow Is Forever*.

Without a doubt Natalie's best-known childhood movie is the 1947 classic *Miracle on 34th Street*, for which she was paid $1,000 a week. She also appeared briefly in an early 1950s television series, *Pride of the Family*.

During her teen years, Natalie blossomed as an actress. Her role opposite the enigmatic James Dean in the 1955 movie *Rebel Without a Cause* won her an Oscar nomination for best supporting actress. The movie is a brilliant evocation of disaffected American teenagers in the 1950s and remains a screen classic. Natalie's allure in the movie was not lost on a young Elvis Presley, who in 1956 could be seen squiring Miss Wood around his hometown of Memphis on the back of his motorcycle.

The following year Natalie married actor Robert Wagner, whom she called RJ. They were divorced only a few years later, but the couple remarried in 1972. Appearing in the 1961 movie *Splendor in the Grass* with Warren Beatty, Natalie projected repressed sexuality so skillfully that she won her second Oscar nomination. That same year she starred as Maria in the film version of *West Side Story*, but singer Marni Nixon was called in to overdub her singing voice.

In the 1960s Natalie was often stereotyped in films as a vulnerable, put-upon woman. Her skill at projecting this image garnered her a third Oscar nomination in 1963 for *Love with the Proper Stranger*. But Natalie knew that she had to change Hollywood's preconceptions of her, and she took on an entirely different persona to star in the controversial 1969 sex farce *Bob & Carol & Ted & Alice*. This movie endures as a record of the kind of sexual experimentation and permissiveness that were in vogue during the 1960s. The year of the movie's release, Natalie married producer Richard Gregson and gave birth to a daughter, Natasha. She and Gregson divorced three years later.

Natalie Wood was a beautiful and talented actress, but some movie critics felt that her performances showed a very limited range of emotions.

The balcony scene in the 1961 movie *West Side Story* is played on a New York fire escape with Natalie Wood as Maria/Juliet and Richard Beymer as Tony/Romeo.

Critics often commented that Natalie seemed happiest as a supporting character rather than as a star in her own movie. She was insecure about her talent and expressed great surprise when a mutual friend told her that the legendary actor Laurence Olivier spoke positively about her work. For most of the 1970s, Natalie kept away from the sound stage, but she appeared in television adaptations of *Cat on a Hot Tin Roof* and *From Here to Eternity*.

After she remarried Robert Wagner in 1972, Natalie seemed content to be raising their brood: Wagner's daughter Kate from his marriage to Marion Marshall, her daughter Natasha, and the Wagners' own daughter, Courtney. When a friend worried aloud about all the time she was losing in her acting career, Natalie simply said, "Hell, I don't really care. I've been a movie star longer than Joan Crawford." By the end of the decade, she was once again on the big screen, appearing in two critically lauded movies, *Willie and Phil* and *The Last Married Couple in America*.

Natalie and RJ often sailed with friends on their 60-foot yacht, *Splendor*. On November 29, 1981, Natalie Wood drowned in a mysterious accident near the boat. While there were whispers about a drinking problem and suicide, her close friends noted that she was looking forward to making her stage debut in a Los Angeles production of *Anastasia* a few months later.

Malcolm X was born Malcolm Little in Omaha, Nebraska, on May 19, 1925. His father was a Baptist preacher who supported Marcus Garvey's Back to Africa movement. When Malcolm was four, the family moved to Lansing, Michigan, where Earl Little planned to run a store while continuing his preaching. A group of white supremacists, who called themselves the Black Legion, learned of Earl's efforts to organize Lansing's black community and became irate. Late one night, while the family slept, the Black Legion set fire to their home. Earl moved his family to East Lansing. When a city ordinance was passed forbidding blacks to leave their homes after sundown, the Littles relocated to a small farmhouse outside of town. Two years later, Earl Little was found dead on the trolley tracks in East Lansing. One side of his head had been crushed, and a streetcar had run over him, severing his body in half. Despite the police department's claim that Earl's death was an accident, Malcolm believed his father was murdered by white supremacists.

Following Earl's death, Louise Little tried unsuccessfully to support her eight children. Unable to find steady work, she applied for general assistance. Malcolm started stealing candy and fruit from neighborhood stores. He was caught several times, and finally, the court decided that Louise was unable to control Malcolm and had him removed from her charge. A couple who knew Malcolm volunteered to take him into their home. Two years later, Louise was committed to a state mental institution, where she remained for 26 years.

After eighth grade Malcolm dropped out of school and traveled to Boston, where his older sister Ella lived. Later, he worked his way to New York City and dramatically changed his appearance. He wore zoot suits and dyed his straightened hair red, earning himself the nickname Detroit Red. To support his growing drug habit, Malcolm sold marijuana, ran numbers, and pimped for prostitutes. After his life was threatened, he was forced to leave New York and return to Boston, where he organized a burglary ring,

1925-1965

This picture of Malcolm X was taken in 1964 around the time when he broke with Elijah Muhammad and the Black Muslims to form his own mosque.

In September 1963 Malcolm X addressed a rally in Harlem. Converting all African Americans to the Muslim movement was his stated ambition.

which the police eventually uncovered. In 1946 Malcolm was sentenced to a 10-year prison term.

Life in prison had an unusual effect on Malcolm X. He used the time to educate himself, spending many hours in the prison library, where he studied history, learned the fundamentals of grammar, and increased his vocabulary. He was also introduced to a new religion, the Nation of Islam. Malcolm's younger brother Reginald, who was already a member, told Malcolm about Allah. Much of what he had to say confused Malcolm, but two phrases took root in his mind: "The white man is the devil," and "the black man is brainwashed."

After talking with his brother, Malcolm reviewed his life. He remembered how his family had been terrorized by white supremacists, the intrusive white social workers who helped commit his mother to a mental institution, his exploitation at the hands of white employers, the harassment he received from white police officers, and the stiff jail sentence passed down by a white judge. Malcolm learned that if he wanted to join the Nation of Islam, he would have to accept its theology and submit completely to the authority of its leader, Elijah Muhammad. Inspired by the new direction his life was taking, Malcolm wrote Elijah Muhammad a heartfelt letter. Elijah Muhammad wrote back, welcoming Malcolm to the faith. He instructed Malcolm to drop his Christian surname, which his ancestors inherited from a white slave owner, and to replace it with the letter X, which symbolized that his true African name had been lost.

In 1952 Malcolm was paroled from prison after serving six years. Rather than returning to crime, Malcolm committed himself to learning more about his new religion. In 1958 he married a Muslim sister named Betty Shabazz. Together they had four children: Daughter Attilah, Daughter Quiblah, Daughter Ilyassah, and Daughter Amilah. Over the next several years, Malcolm developed into one of the Nation of Islam's most powerful speakers, attracting thousands of African Americans to the fold. Malcolm's charismatic personality also attracted the attention of the white media. Unlike Dr. Martin Luther King Jr., who believed in nonviolent tactics to achieve equal rights for blacks, Malcolm favored the use of arms and proposed a revolutionary program that would create a separate society for blacks. Malcolm's relationship with the media displeased Elijah Muhammad. He felt the Nation of Islam's message was being overshadowed by Malcolm's newfound celebrity.

Malcolm was alarmed by reports that paternity suits were being filed against Elijah Muhammad by two women who had previously worked as his secretaries. Anxious to get to the root of the rumors, Malcolm met with the two women. They confirmed that Elijah had fathered their children. They

At a 1963 rally Malcolm X holds up a current copy of the Black Muslim newspaper *Muhammad Speaks*.

On March 26, 1964, during the Senate filibuster against the civil rights bill, Malcolm X and Dr. Martin Luther King Jr. shook hands, following King's press conference in the Capitol.

also warned Malcolm to be cautious in his dealings with Elijah Muhammad because he had predicted that Malcolm would one day turn against him. In a private meeting with Malcolm, Elijah Muhammad did not deny the accusations. Instead, he justified his behavior by comparing himself with such biblical figures as David and Noah, who also suffered moral lapses. Elijah's response left Malcolm dissatisfied and contributed to his growing disenchantment with the Nation of Islam.

In November 1963 Malcolm's candidness with reporters provided Elijah with an excuse to sideline him. Referring to President Kennedy's assassination, Malcolm called the murder a case of "the chickens coming home to roost." The public was outraged by Malcolm's comments, prompting Elijah Muhammad to relieve him of his duties for 90 days. Feeling betrayed by the Nation of Islam, Malcolm decided not to return. He announced plans to organize his own movement to be called Muslim Mosque, Incorporated. It was based in New York City and had about fifty charter members. Malcolm told the media that the organization's goals were to "eliminate the political oppression, the economic exploitation, and the social degradation suffered daily by 22 million Afro-Americans." He invited blacks everywhere to join him in his new crusade. In response to Malcolm's announcement, Elijah Muhammad wrote in his biweekly newspaper, "Only those who wish to be led to hell, or to their doom, will follow Malcolm." In the next few months, several attempts were made on Malcolm's life. This did not surprise him: "No one can get out without trouble. This thing with me will be resolved by death and violence."

In April 1964 Malcolm made a pilgrimage to Mecca, the Islamic holy city. The trip had a profound effect on him. He was greeted warmly by Muslims of all nationalities, including white Eurasians. Malcolm realized that true brotherhood included "people of all races, colors, from all over the world coming together as one. It has proved to me the power of One God." In an open letter to the press describing his pilgrimage, Malcolm wrote that he was "spellbound by the graciousness I see displayed all around me by people of all colors." In the future Malcolm would judge people by their words and actions, not by the pigment of their skin.

On Sunday, February 21, 1965, at 2:00 P.M., Malcolm arrived at the Audubon Ballroom in Harlem, where he held weekly meetings. Four hundred people were already seated, waiting to hear his address. Facing his audience, Malcolm uttered a traditional Muslim greeting, "Asaikum, brothers and sisters!" Suddenly, a disturbance broke out several rows back. "Get your hands out of my pockets!" a man shouted. "Don't be messing with my pockets!" Meanwhile, a man stood up in the front row. He lifted a sawed-off shotgun and fired a shot into Malcolm's chest. At that same moment, two other armed men appeared in the aisle and also fired shots at him.

While the assailants fled, several aides rushed to Malcolm's side. He was taken to a hospital, but Malcolm X was already dead. Outside the ballroom one of the gunmen, Talmadge Hayer, was apprehended by police. Although the Nation of Islam was suspected of being behind Malcolm's murder, Hayer denied having any involvement with the organization. He also claimed not to know the other two gunmen, who were also convicted of the murder.

A week before he was murdered, Malcolm X returned to New York from Great Britain, where he and a BBC news team had visited the town of Smethwick, which at that time barred blacks.

LD KAREN CARPENTER HARRY CHAPIN

ERTO CLEMENTE PATSY CLINE EDDIE CO

LTRANE SAM COOKE JIM CROCE BOBE

OMINIQUE DUNNE CASS ELLIOT PERRY

ER WERNER FASSBINDER F. SCOTT FITZGERA

LOWELL GEORGE JIMI HENDRIX JIM HENS

BRIAN JONES JANIS JOPLIN JOHN KENNE

RTIN LUTHER KING JR. ERNIE KOVACS BR

RD JAYNE MANSFIELD ROBERT MAPPLETH

A MCAULIFFE GLENN MILLER SAL MINE

KEITH MOON JIM MORRISON THURMA

PHIL OCHS CHRISTINA ONASSIS CHARL

LVIS PRESLEY FREDDIE PRINZE GILDA RA

TCH DEL SHANNON RITCHIE VALENS

ATS WALLER HANK WILLIAMS DENNIS